# Rock Bottom

Beyond Drug Addiction

by

**Members of the Arta Rehabilitation Centre**
**Aalt van den Berg et al**

Translated by Jacob Cornelis

Hawthorn Press

Published by Hawthorn Press,
Bankfield House, 13 Wallbridge, Stroud GL5 3JA
English translation © 1987 Hawthorn Press
Translated from the Dutch, *Verslaving Arta, Jaargang 49 Nv1, January 1986,*
of the *Vrije Opvoedkunst* magazine.

No part of this book may be reproduced in any form without permission from the publisher, except for the quotation of brief passages for fair criticism and comment.

Cover design by Patrick Roe, Glevum Graphics

Typeset in Plantin by Q Set, 2 Conway Road, Gloucester
Printed by Billings & Son Ltd, Worcester

**Acknowledgements**

Grateful acknowledgements for editorial assistance are made to Ruth Manson, by Jakob Cornelis; to Shirley Routledge of the *Itâ Wegman Foundation* which contributed to the translation, and to Tijno Voors who has encouraged an awareness of Arta's work in the U.K.

**British Library Cataloguing in Publication Data**

Bergetal, A. van den
   Rock bottom : beyond drug addiction. —
   (Social ecology series).
   1. Drug abuse
   I. Title II. Series
   362.2'93    RC564
   ISBN 1–86989–011–6

# Contents

| | | |
|---|---|---|
| **Foreword** | *Dr Derek Blincow* | page v |
| **Introduction** | | page vii |
| **Chapter 1**<br>What is addiction? | *Marko van Gerven* | page 1 |
| **Chapter 2**<br>Addiction as an aspect of the quest for self-knowledge | *Jaap van der Haar* | page 5 |
| **Chapter 3**<br>How can we understand the causes of drug use? | *Cees van Lelieveld* | page 9 |
| **Chapter 4**<br>Could threshold experiences cause drug use? | *Sjon van Schaick* | page 16 |
| **Chapter 5**<br>Arta and its residents | *Margit Ilgen* | page 24 |
| **Chapter 6**<br>Addiction from the point of view of parents | *Peter Scheers* | page 33 |
| **Chapter 7**<br>Aftercare: A social remedy . . . or remedy for society? | *Aalt van den Berg* | page 37 |
| **Chapter 8**<br>Aftercare facilities | *Sjon van Schaick* | page 43 |
| **Chapter 9**<br>What are drugs? How do they work? and what are the effects of their use? | *Ron Dunselman* | page 45 |
| **References** | | page 55 |
| **Appendix I**<br>The Elements of Human Life | *Dr Derek Blincow* | page 56 |
| **Appendix II**<br>Contacts | | page 61 |

# Foreword

*Dr Derek Blincow*

What follows is a working document: A variety of contributions that generate a picture of drug dependency which can unfold a meaning for individual development.

I do not think many of us would readily link the two. In the past twenty years or so we have become much more objective about the 'drug problem'; recognizing symptoms of drug dependence, withdrawal syndromes, tolerance, drug-related problems. We have begun to conceive of drug dependence as an 'illness', and the whole area has lost those moralising tones of earlier times, certainly for workers in the field. Research continues to explore these aspects in ever greater detail, and yet, when we come to look for a remedy for the addicts themselves, we are faced with the need to address quite different issues.

Drugs, as the 'user' rapidly discovers, are not merely substances. They speak to us on many different levels. For some the immediate effects may be unpleasant, frightening, and even downright disastrous. For a sizeable minority, however, drugs provide a ready-made, reliable and effective panacea for every ill. Such users begin to value their drugs and will go to great lengths to get them. Indeed, the usual course is for all else to pale into insignificance. Extra finance is needed, deals must be struck, soon all sorts of other dependencies are established and the addict, for that is what the individual has now become, enters a much darker world. The drug that began life as a good friend is now ticket to a nightmare.

For those of you who have been touched or directly affected by addictive behaviour these nightmare aspects will be deeply familiar. It is not for nothing that Alcoholics Anonymous developed the concept of 'rock bottom'; meaning that point of lowest descent, isolated, debilitated, manipulating all around, the individual's life out of control, an utter blackness. For some it is the deterioration in their physical health which calls a halt, for others the disasters in their relationships, yet others the disasters they cause around them. Tales of neglect, callousness and outrageously irresponsible acts abound amongst these folk, and it can and does lead to violence, injury, and death. The black is often very black indeed.

Rock bottom, however, has another meaning. As much as it reflects back on a darkening descent, it also provides the basis for a total revolution in the individual's life. A decided part of this revolution is overcoming the physical need for the drug, which we know as withdrawal. But it would be very wrong to assume that, once the drug has left the body and bodily functions have returned to more normal activities, the addict is 'cured'. We know for example that the physical withdrawal from opiate drugs (heroin, morphine etc.) takes roughly four to seven days, but there is a sort of emotional paralysis, a gripping fear that many, if not all, suffer and this may go on for months. There is an inability to discriminate, to reflect, to judge, and to decide which persists much longer. Those who recover say that to work through all these stages it takes years.

Research in this whole field is extremely problematic, for the process we observe is for the most part not readily measurable. How, after all, do we identify deficits in our emotional life, in our relationships with others, in the ability to take on and sustain a responsible independence? And when we add to this the attainment in adulthood of the maturer human capacities of faith, love, and hope, the task seems quite hopeless and we are left either totally abandoning the effort or attempting to reduce the sweep and richness of such concepts to number and statistical manipulation. But it is just these emotional, interpersonal, and, dare I say, spiritual qualities that are the vital factors in whether this process we are describing will be fulfilled.

One of the great values of the contributions that follow is their search for an objective and yet faithful understanding of just such a developmental process. They have attempted to reflect their experience by means of concepts which for many may be new, foreign, and provocative. The terms they use stem in large measure from the work and lectures given by Dr. Rudolf Steiner in the early part of this century. The image of the human being he presented is deservedly complex, claims to be comprehensive, and, from my own experience, is frustratingly opaque to a purely intellectual appraisal.

I do not think we should be put off by this. After all, to understand the human being in human terms should by rights require the fullest range of our abilities. Nevertheless a brief account of this image of the human being is given on page 56 for readers to refer to.

# Introduction

*Arta* is a rehabilitation centre for drug addicts in Holland. It accommodates twenty five 'residents'. In addition, about fifty people are involved in a follow-up program, including former residents, co-workers, volunteers and employers.

According to the health authorities in Holland, which subsidise Arta, the approach of this institution is notable in two respects:
- The methods and arrangements for aftercare are unique in Holland;
- Fifty two percent of the residents who enter the Arta program following the withdrawal phase stay off drugs permanently after leaving. The national average is 10% to 15%.

It should be noted that those entering Arta are in no way different from those entering other therapeutic communities in terms of background, education, etc.

This series of articles was an outcome of a number of talks given by Arta co-workers for the upper classes of several Waldorf Schools in Holland and Belgium. It appeared that there was much interest in, and confusion about, drugs – also on the part of parents and teachers. They all asked questions such as:
- Why do young people get into drugs?
- Which drugs are there, and what are the consquences of using them?
- What is addiction?
- What is done about this at Arta?

The treatment of drug addiction and rehabilitation of drug addicts are new fields. There are few people with much more than ten years' experience. Much, if not everything, has to be started from scratch. Only gradually is the experience and understanding of the problems involved growing wider.

These articles, which originally appeared in *Vrije Opvoedkunst**, the official periodical of the *Vereniging voor Vrije Opvoedkunst* (Association for Free [Waldorf] Pedagogy) in Holland, present some initial ideas of the authors, based on their early experiences related to drug addiction. Each contribution represents a particular personal perspective and interest. An attempt has been made, however, to form a unity. It is a 'debut'. Everything is still in development, including the contributors!

* Vol. 49, No. 1 – January 1986.

# Chapter 1

# What is addiction?

*Marko van Gerven*

Addiction to drugs, alcohol, or medications constitutes one of the most prominent problems in our society. The media pay much attention to the social aspects of the drug question, such as young people suffering from overdoses, or neighbourhoods rendered unsafe because of crime and prostitution. Alcohol draws less attention, although the consequences of alcohol use are much more serious (traffic accidents; hospitalization as a result of injury or illness related to alcohol use: disorderly conduct in public places, or marital disputes with violence). What receives least attention is addiction to so-called medication, which for the most part involves 'nice' people, who do not need to resort to theft in order to get what they need, but acquire it by means of a doctor's prescription. This last form of addiction is perhaps the most prevalent, and shows, in our society, a strong tendency to benumb consciousness.

Addiction is something that involves the whole human being. It has a psychological, a biographical, and a social aspect. One could also say that addiction is an attack on the human 'I'. Serious as that may be in itself, it is still not so easy to determine when there actually is an addiction problem. Someone may be addicted for a long time without anyone noticing it. When a form of addiction is regarded as socially acceptable, use may be continued for years without being seen as a problem. It is interesting to note that the use of so-called hard or soft drugs is viewed rather as socially deviant behaviour, or may be regarded as a challenge to accepted social norms. Perhaps much of the fear related to drugs is related to a lack of courage to let go of the apparent certainties of our visible world.

While 'the' problem, therefore, is difficult to delineate, I will nevertheless attempt to give a picture of the damaging effects of addiction. I, too, consider addiction one of the most intense and serious illnesses anyone can have. In the light of my work, I consider a tolerant social attitude towards addiction dangerous. This attitude deprives the addict of the possibility of experiencing significant crisis events in his life.

Experience indicates that at times of adversity, such as illness, arrest, departure of a friend, a feeling can arise in an individual that he/she can not go on this way. This feeling is commonly the starting point for seeking to make a change in one's life situation. What then arises is a first, unconscious yearning to be loved again by another, and ultimately to regain one's self-respect.

**Three aspects of addiction**

1. Addiction is brought about by means of a poison. Traditionally, poisons have played an important role in medicine and in religious practices. Each poison has in principle a dual effect: it releases forces in the body that are experienced as intoxication, as a 'kick', or as hallucination: these are the metabolic forces that are needed, however, to regenerate and restore normal bodily functions, and as a result of ingesting the poison, physical weakness occurs, as well as a slowing down of the bodily functions and a lowering of the body temperature. Forms of illness can also result that appear to have as a common factor the disturbance of the biological recognition of one's own body, which is one of the functions of the ego. A special condition arises with respect to poison, which is expressed under the term 'dependence'. The body gets used to the poison, which is why the addict needs an ever-larger dose to get the desired effect. This also brings about the dreaded effects of withdrawal. Withdrawal phenomena resemble a general revolt of the body, with tears, running nose, diarrhoea, insomnia, chills, irritation, restlessness and pains throughout the body being some of the most familiar symptoms. The most serious of these, incidentally, fade away after a few days.

2. The human soul functions are thinking, feeling, and willing. The thinking becomes obsessed by the poison. The user talks about it constantly with other users, and is occupied with looking for legal as well as illegal sources for it. Obviously, because of this strong craving, moral strictures are easily ignored. The 'high' is a relatively short, pleasant interlude, after which the same vicious circle starts again.

The emotional life of the user becomes shallow and indifferent. Relatives and friends are cheated; they are told all kinds of fishy stories to obtain money. Social contacts are dominated by the importance of the 'stuff'. Because of this, relations with non-addicts become less important. This isolation reinforces a tendency to join a user sub-culture (the 'scene'). It becomes more and more difficult to maintain lasting relationships: a partner is also cheated, or, if possible dragged into it as well.

In the life of will, paralysis sets in. Agreements are forgotten, or not honoured. Keeping a job or coping with adversity becomes more and more difficult.

3. When one studies the history of an addict, one often notices a regrettable sequence of missed opportunities on the part of parents, and doctors. There is a pattern. In childhood there was often severe tension between the parents, with quarrels, violence, and drinking. Frequently the parents separated early on, with a number of different people subsequently caring for the child at one time or another. At school there were behavioural problems, such as playing hookie or truanting, wandering about on the streets, unrest in the classroom, lack of concentration, problems, directly related to the atmosphere at home. During puberty there were conflicts with educators over restrictions (dress, choice of friends); teachers and schools often took a hard-line position, which resulted either in compliance only for appearance's sake, or in further escalation of the conflict.

After repeated disasters the addicted child drops out of school and goes looking for satisfaction in a sub-culture – the use of hash, speed or alcohol then starts in earnest.

The failure of a relationship is for many drug users the starting point for a serious escalation of addictive behaviour. Poisons then also become a form of consolation, a means of forgetting depression and anxiety. Criminality and prostitution wait at the bottom of a downward spiral.

**Encounter**

From the above it should be clear that addiction is an attack on the ability to live one's own life. The essence of any turn-around must be sought in the first instance in the sort of human encounter that stirs something inwardly. In every human being there lives the activity of the higher 'I', which helps one in one's human encounters. Because of that which someone else can awaken in one, there comes to life a first recognition of one's own capacities, aspirations, and ideals. This generates the initial warmth, the spark that can once again light a fire. One person, or one meeting, is usually not enough. There is often regression because the distortions are too great, the ego force too weak. A community such as Arta can be a help in offering the opportunity to experience many encounters. These are encounters that in principle must include all three of the levels mentioned previously: nourishment, change, and direction for life. It is a touching and gratifying task to be able to participate in the first few steps in this direction. We, as non-users, can experience what addiction can teach us about our current social disease.

# Chapter 2

# Addiction as an aspect of the quest of self-knowledge

*Jaap van der Haar*

In the practice of contemporary scientific research, phenomena are to an increasing degree investigated in isolation by specialists. It is not surprising, therefore, that this same tendency can be found in the investigation of the causes underlying addiction. This only removes the problem from the totality of its social context, and causes it to be considered as no more than inappropriate behaviour. From this follows a model for treatment aimed at correcting the inappropriate behaviour of the addict after he has been isolated from society. By means of punishment and reward, the addict is encouraged to break off poor behaviour and learn good behaviour. This is the model. This is how he attains to a respectively lower or higher status in the therapeutic community. The tensions this adaptation process creates can be released in regular group sessions – e.g., with yelling and screaming.

This particular interpretation of the problem of addiction does not appear to lead to any effective solutions. The starting point – namely that addiction is 'inappropriate behaviour that can be corrected' – turns out, in practice, to be inadequate.

There are more and more question marks about the efficacy of such therapeutic communities for drug addicts. Besides, according to the research of the last few years, it has been frequently shown that psychopathocological disorders of a highly depressive nature are often at the root of the phenomenon of addiction.

As a result, there is more and more acceptance of the idea that addiction belongs in psychiatric departments, i.e., that it must be isolated and treated by specialists.

Socially, the problem is seen as insoluble, which diverts attention from the socio-cultural context in which the problem originated to begin with.

In spite of all this, it turns out that on a small scale surprising results are being obtained in the therapy of drug addicts. It is notable that in these instances addiction is seen neither as a purely individual, nor a purely social problem, but as an aspect of the entire cultural situation of today, of which every one of us is a part.

It is not so easy to convince others of this viewpoint. To do so requires that one relinquish the idea that human consciousness has always been the same as it is today. When this is done, it then becomes possible to acquire new perspectives with respect to the problem of addiction. These can, indeed, point to a viable solution of this problem.

As stated, the starting point for this is that human consciousness, and the culture that gives expression to this consciousness, has been subject to change over time. In the pre-Grecian, ancient Egyptian culture man experienced the outer world in a dreamlike way, but at the same time in a way that was rich in impressions. Only gradually did he develop the capacity and the need to have knowledge of the world with an awake, individual consciousness.

It was more than 2000 years ago, during the heyday of the culture of ancient Greece, that individual human thought first unfolded. Many of the viewpoints formulated in this Greek culture later became the basis for the social order subsequently spread across Europe by the Romans.

From the Greek era on, man has focussed on getting to know the world through thought. In the process he has developed a valuable and fruitful scientific method with which to comprehend himself and the world. One basic premise is that only that which is perceptible through the physical senses and, therefore, verifiable, is real.

It would be illogical, however, to assume that this has brought man to the end of the development of consciousness. Just as the idea that only the physically perceptible is real is in fact a hypothesis, so there has to be the possibility of another basic premise – hypothetical, to be sure – that besides the physically perceptible world there is another world that is not of the physical kind. Using our thinking as an organ of perception we can get to know this world, too. Natural scientific thought, therefore, must be questioned in as far as it forms the basis for an approach to the problem of addiction because, in view of the results, this approach is not very effecive.

An irresistible need for human self-knowledge is growing, apparently spontaneously, at the present. Even though the scientific tendency still is to look only at the physical, sense-perceptible world, it is more and more apparent that the individual human being is asking questions about his own 'invisible' origin and about his own 'inner world'.

Our culture has responded readily to these questions. Old meditative paths toward self-knowledge are again being brought to our attention. Courses are offered with the aim of fathoming the significance of the course our own lives are taking. 'Retreat' weekends are available in profusion.

At the same time, the number of people who (unconsciously) reject this is also growing. Their aim is not self-knowledge; on the contrary, it is lowering of consciousness. Drug addicts, although they receive a lot of attention, are but a small part of this group. As compared to 40,000 registered hard-drug addicts in The Netherlands, there are 400,000 registered alcoholics, and a much larger number of daily users of tranquillizers, not to mention the many who seek 'oblivion' through radio, television and one-armed bandits

The development of human consciousness, as briefly characterized above, has thus far led to much useful knowledge of the sense-perceptible world. This knowledge leads to a certain kind of relationship to the world – we can observe this in the development of every child. That which remains unknown elicits fear. The tendency is to stay away from it. When, however, we find the courage to approach the unknown, we can be led to the knowledge with which problems can be solved.

On the one hand, a need is apparent in modern man to get to know himself; on the other hand, our culture appears to be full of opportunities to turn away from oneself, to become addicted to the means of diminishing one's consciousness.

The answer to the problem of addiction, therefore, has to be sought in a path to self-knowledge suitable for modern man.

When the tendency to take flight (from oneself) is thus regarded as a cultural sign of the times, it becomes obvious that a solution can not be found only in institutionalized therapeutic communities. These can offer help in extreme cases, but society as a whole must come up with an answer that will penetrate the entire cultural fabric.

It is understandable that rejection is the first reaction to such an idea. For acceptance would mean that the problem of addiction could no longer be kept at arm's length and left to experts. The solution then would have far-reaching social consequences that are everybody's concern, specifically, how we bring up and educate our children.

Pedagogy and education would not in the first place have the aim of producing what is now referred to as 'functional social behaviour'. Rather, they would seek to accompany the child in the unfolding of his/her own distinctive personality in such a way that in adulthood the individual would be able to find his own relation to his own being and to the world. This further implies that possibly he might not go along with the cultural, social, and economic viewpoints embedded in our society.

The necessity of finding a broad social response to the tendency to seek escape, and the role pedagogy and education can play in this, becomes clear through the fact that in the great majority of cases hard-drug use starts between the ages of 17 and 18. This is when the individual personality is born, as it were. This is when the fear of getting to know the world and the self through one's own powers begins to manifest itself. This fear is real enough when up-bringing and education have failed to provide the necessary foundations on which to base the shaping of one's own life.

These viewpoints derive from the spiritual-scientific developmental psychology on which Steiner* education and the therapeutic program of Arts are based (see the contribution from Margit Ilgen). The validity of these viewpoints is demonstrated by their practical results. Of all those who over the past seven years were admitted to the therapeutic community of Arta, fifty two percent were able to take their own lives in hand without drugs. For those communities based on behavioural therapies the corresponding percentage is ten or fifteen.

These results make it clear how important it is to develop new points of view that can lead to a broad social response to the growing tendency to addiction in today's social environment.

* Steiner education and Waldorf education are used interchangeably. Rudolf Steiner was the founder of the first Waldorf school.

# Chapter 3

# How can we understand the causes of drug use?

*Cees van Lelieveld*

**Introduction**

The enormous increase in drug use since the Sixties raises many questions – among others, what are the causes of this phenomenon? It seems to us that what is going on is an interaction between the individual (family, school) and the spirit of the time (the age of consciousness soul, threshold experiences).

The process of human individuation is going forward, hand in hand with a fading away, and sometimes disappearance, of a supportive enveloping social fabric. In the life before birth, in the family, and at school, much can take place that has a rigidifying effect on the later soul development of the young person. Deep down, he feels out of sorts. All around is emptiness and boredom. This can at the same time be seen as a hunger of the soul.

Drugs give the appearance of giving an answer to this longing of the developing soul. It is not a true answer, however, neither with respect to the emptiness, nor to the pain the soul has experienced in the family, in school, or in society at large. Rather, what has to be done is to find the source of this emptiness, which can be seen as a deep longing of man – although this is not grasped – to be understood in his deepest essence, and to come to terms with the strongly negative experiences which, having often been 'put away' in the subconscious, begin to lead a life of their own. Is it a break-through of the spirit that counts, in the final analysis?

In this chapter we want to discuss soul development and the possible disturbances within the individual that may occur in the course of life.

* * *

# Soul development and possible disturbances within the individual

## 1. Experiences in the family and in school

To a great extent, that which the human being becomes, and is capable of in later life is related to his development in earliest childhood, at birth, and during the existence before birth. Only at about age seven has the child built up his body out of what was inherited (all cellular material having undergone complete turnover.) Children's diseases play an important role in this formative process, the objective being to make a better 'home' for the self or ego. Of the greatest importance at this time are a protective environment, warmth, love, and trust. This is what helps healthy psychological physical development. Trust, once experienced, can later grow into self-confidence. Example and imitation are central to early childhood education. Everything that enters via the senses has a formative effect.

*Disturbances:* Everyone can appreciate that it makes a great deal of difference whether or not a child is wanted. Marital conflict, discord, and aggression have a *direct* effect on the organism of the child. So does premature intellectual development (before the child is ready for school). Much damage is done when colours, images, sounds, and nutrition are not fully adapted to the young child. It is difficult to catch up later with what is neglected at this early age. The person in question carries this neglect with him. To accept this is really the only way he can later actively give form to his own Life.

In the second period of seven years, when the life body is born, the transformation of the acquired (imitated) tendencies, habits, and temperament takes place. The soul life remains sheltered, albeit less so. Loving authority is of great importance in this period. It engenders reverence and respect. The reverence for a person later grows into a strong striving after, and longing for, truth. The life of feeling develops through being presented with parables, metaphors, and images of great historical figures.

*Disturbances:* In this period the school plays an important role beside the parents. What can have a disturbing effect is the failure of the child to find a sufficient degree of loving authority, or receiving little or no nourishment for the development of its life of feeling. Around age nine or ten there arises the first experience of the self confronting the world (a new manifestation of the ego). This is accompanied by feelings of loneliness and sorrow. The question is then whether the parents can turn to the child lovingly, which prepares the child's heart for the birth of a soul life of its own (from age thirteen on). In this period, traumatic experiences can occur for children – for instance, incest experiences.

## 2. Soul development as such

As we shall see, disturbances may occur in the child's own developing soul life (from age fourteen on) that may form the basis for addiction. These disturbances relate to those that may already have occurred in the first and second seven-year periods.

What is typical of the third seven-year period is this: Around age twelve, the capacity to conceptualize and to think abstractly come to the fore (which has to do with the fact that the head has already lost much of its 'life'). The capacity for abstract thought is in polar opposition to a new kind of life in the metabolic system. On the one hand, the teenager is 'thinking smart' in confronting the world, is given to abstraction; on the other hand, he is prone to 'gut reactions' – passionate, emotional, sometimes compulsive. Cool, slack in attitude, apathetic on the one hand; on the other hand impulsively active. Withdrawn one moment, and conquering the world the next. Jung called this the dualistic phase. The loosening of the ties with the parents goes hand in hand with the child's loosening of his own soul from the mother's protection.

With sexual maturity, a new relation to the earth comes about. Desire for the partner lives in the soul of the adolescent boy. This is less so for girls because they maintain a lively connection with their feelings.

Between the poles of withdrawal in cool observation and of desire for participation in the world lies the possibility for breathing in living experiences. These experiences can arise only when the desires directed at the outside world and aloof observation are brought into connection. From the intense observation of a sunset, one retains certain experience. The experience of sympathy for another person frees the soul: I approach him/her. These experiences and encounters are the life blood of the adolescent soul. Judgments can then arise out of the full human being, from a lively feeling life and from the will. From these, individualized concepts may be formed – the sixteen- or 17-year-old starts to think for him/herself, and asks:
What is true? What is good? What is beautiful? Thus a path is found from dark desire to interest and interpreting one's own impressions (judgments, concepts, understanding).

It is of decisive importance in this period to arouse interest in the world. During the second half of this period, young persons can form ideals of their own that can fill their hearts.

*Disturbances:* The young person's own soul life can be either too weak or can unfold too forcefully. A weak soul life means underdevelopment; the teenager gives an impression of being younger than his age, and relating back to an earlier period. This can become apparent in a strong tendency to conform to what he sees in the environment, or to lean on authority. Becoming more independent from the parents, forming one's own thoughts and ideals, are things that take place only partially. The development of feeling and will are retarded.

When the soul life has too strong an influence, the problems related to puberty are aggravated. The polarity between thinking and willing is magnified, and the middle (feeling) is inaccessible. A critical attitude becomes over-critical, and even leads to rejection. Sexual desire is strong, but unconnected to love. Desire seeks satisfaction devoid of love. Here, too, the soul life as such – development of a feeling life – lags behind, overpowered as it is by desires.

Let us consider this development in more detail:

In the case of the teenager who has remained childish the soul quickly becomes exhausted and weak. Too much soul force, on the other hand, results in an uncontrolled emotional life surging forth, which may find release in aggression and anger. Both cases result in cramping. The immature boy or girl reacts by wanting to act too strongly on the body, and gets a cramp, which leads to high blood pressure. When the soul has too strong an influence, headaches and migraine can result. In some cases, the person can overcome these disturbances, but perhaps only with help.

A living inner experience, in both cases, lags behind. The general complaint is about a lack of feeling, or about inner emptiness which traces back to a lack of feeling. This can go so far as an experience of rigidity, even of death (suicide). In such cases, these young people have very little feeling for whatever is offered in the way of beautiful impressions. What is happening is that desires are not connected with observations – the latter leave them cold. Only in relating observation to desire can feeling arise. It may also be that the feeling that is aroused in undifferentiated; everything is "right on, man," often expressed in a monotone. What this comes down to is a failure to relate desire to the world in a conscious way, based on interest (interest can usually be aroused eventually; everybody has something that captivates him, which then becomes a starting point for development). Only when inner experience becomes real is there any possibility to digest one's impressions. This is needed for the renewal and enrichment of one's feeling life.

Both these forms of soul disturbance can lead to addiction, which only aggravates the condition (for instance, experiences of prostitution both for boys and girls). Addiction is approximately twice as common for boys as it is for girls. The latter, as already indicated, keep more actively in

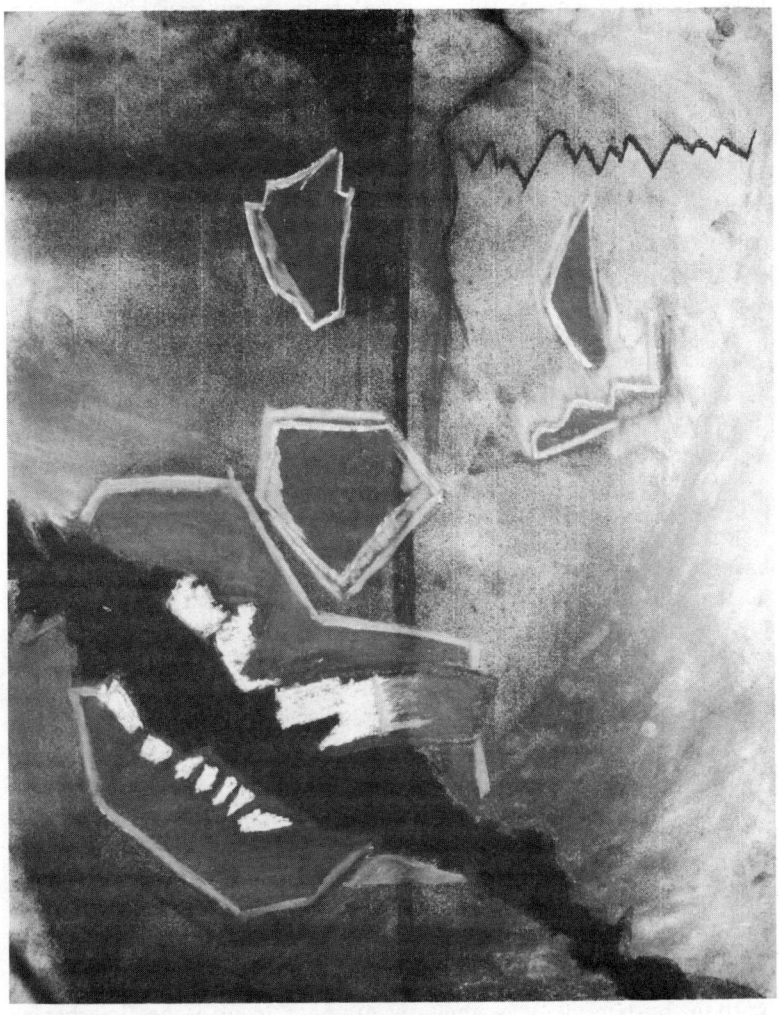

... short-circuit ... speechlessness ... oral death ...   Drawing: Pieter Groen

touch with their feelings during and after puberty anyway, which means that the disturbances described earlier do not occur as commonly for girls.

Thus the immature teenager, with his weak soul activity, can get a craving for the stronger soul experiences provided by drugs. He may also have an urge to join, or submit to, a group. Sometimes it is a case of testing one's courage, or childish curiosity.

In the case of an 'excess of puberty', the incentive is the escape afforded by drugs from the chaos of soul forces with which he can not cope. One may hear the following about the *initial* effect of heroin: "It was something else! All my problems dissolved into nothing. I started to feel OK!"

One can then expect severe conflict situations – protest against parents, school and establishment.

Eventually, a drastic loss of the feeling life of the middle sphere can occur (in men this may be more likely than in women).

The development questions indicated above, and in particular the disturbances mentioned here, which are probably occurring more and more frequently, *can* lead to drug use, and eventually to drug addiction. In many cases, however, it will never happen, or it may be a case of only a temporary encounter with drugs. This is to say that development problems are only part of the complex of causes of drug use.

It is my feeling that guilt reactions on the part of parents, when this background is recognized, are unavoidable, but that this does not have to be the end of it. Much of what may have happened may have been unconscious, or may have been the result of falling back into previous errors, even though they had already been recognized earlier. The pain caused by remembering such past events may be less severe, but it is still there. It can be shared with others, however. In the present, a new relationship can be formed on the basis of a new turn of events in the life of the parents as well as of the addict. For the latter, too, it is not a case of leaving it at that. One must come to terms with the deep wounds in the life of the soul, for instance by means of curative artistic work.

After all, the shaping of a new future must be based on acceptance of what has previously taken place.

**Disturbances in individuation whilst becoming an adult**

With the birth of the 'I' (at about twenty-one), many of the disturbances in development until then can be overcome. A decision to kick a drug habit is relatively rare before this age.

At about age eighteen or nineteen, the birth constellation reoccurs, independent of heredity and cultural environment (the moon node at eighteen years, seven months)*.

At this time, the intentions for one's current incarnation on earth can once again make themselves apparent. It is about this time – according to our observation – that the transition from soft drugs to heroin takes place. There is, in any event, an intensification of drug use, including the reckless use of combination of drugs. Against this background addiction can be viewed as a serious disruption of the individuation process.

Since the individuation impulse works on far into the twenties, a connection can be re-established when the habit has been kicked (this is recognizeable in strongly religious feelings).

Five years ago, during an information meeting at a school about drugs, I heard, for the first time, the life story of a former Arta resident. What impressed me deeply in this story was the possibility of an incarnation process that passes *through* addiction. Mysteriously, the user seems to find a way to the earth right through the very depths of drug use.

1) This article is based on several chapters of *Die Entwicklung der Seele im Lebenslauf* by Rudolf Treichler (Verlag Freies Geistesleben). Also referred to is *Man on the Threshold*, Bernard Lievegoed (Hawthorn Press), 1984.

* While we can speak of seven year rhythms in terms of the births of the various bodies of the human being, there are also other effective rhythmic cycles which retain an echo in human development ed c.f. B.C.J. Lievegoed, *Man on the Threshold*, Hawthorn Press 1984, pp 55-57.

# Chapter 4

# Could threshold experiences cause drug use?

*Sjon van Schaik*

In this contribution we will look at possible causes of drug use from another angle, namely from that of threshold experiences.

We make the assumption that it is possible to gain entry from the material world into the spiritual world. This makes it necessary to form a far more concrete picture of the spiritual world than we are accustomed to. Often we imagine the spiritual world as a world that is far away above us. All too often we are still stuck with the old Christian image of heaven and earth.

For this chapter, however, we have to imagine the spiritual world to be something that is present here and now, directly all round us. The only thing is, we can not see it. Between the material world and the spiritual world there is a threshold, with the result that we can see one, but not the other. This has its basis in our constitution. Our constitution protects us from crossing this threshold. This protection is necessary because the spiritual world is subject to laws and forces that are different from those valid in the material world, and because with our present capacities and limitations we can not cope with these spiritual laws and forces.

It is, in fact, possible for people to cross the threshold, but this leads to what we know as psychiatric syndromes. To be healthy, in this context, means that one can not cross the threshold, while being ill may mean that one can.

There are many signs, however, that indicate that this is changing. Steiner, Lievegoed,* and others, show that the constitution of the human being has been changing in such a way since 1900 (the end of Kali-Yuga) that the threshold is becoming more permeable without causing illness directly. Among others this is observable in the youth of the present day. We do not have to see anything extraordinary in this; typically, it simply means that reality and non-reality intermingle. We can see this in the many ways that adolescents express themselves, such as in drawings, stories, pronouncements, etc., in which the most striking aspect is this: everything is possible.

Below follow two examples – one an excerpt from a story told by a sixteen-year old boy, and the other a drawing by a nineteen-year old boy. It is remarkable how both of these forms of expression came about. The writer says about his story that it flowed from his pen 'just like that' while doing homework, and that he had no idea of how it would end. The artist says: "I started with one sheet of paper, and only wanted to draw a head (of a large being), but it went on and on, and finally I needed nine sheets, and it ended up being one metre by 75 centimetres."
Quotation:

'We were driven to the back of the alley, and it was a dead-end. About seven farmers barred the way to freedom. To our surprise it turned out there was an iron door in the blind wall, half hidden in darkness. We had no choice: either we fell into the hands of the farmers, or we could hurl ourselves against the door. We did the latter, and luckily the door opened. Before the farmers had a chance to grab us we had disappeared behind the door, bicycles and all.

'There was a strange contrast between the racket of the farmers outside and the heavy, dead silence of the corridor in which we were now standing. Almost solemnly, which seemed absurd while pushing a bicycle, we walked through the eerie passage, our steps softened in the centimetre-thick carpet. The corridor seemed endless. It seemed to disappear into nothingness – ceiling and walls melting one into the other, the chandeliers floating strangely in the passage, shining quietly. Neither of us dared to speak, afraid of our own voices. Maria, who led the way, looked back at every step to see if I was still there. We passed through several meaningless doors, after each of which the corridor continued unchanged, doors and passages, until suddenly the next passage was different, descending. The floor as well as the ceiling and walls were red. Plain, painfully bright red – even the walls, ceiling and floor indistinguishable. It was as if you walked in a space that swallowed you up, everything was red, including even Maria's brightly shining teeth. I read in her large-red eyes what I knew to be in mine: desperation. 'Let's go back,' she said in a near-whisper, 'anything is better than this; rather the pulling rope of the village than having to walk on to the end here.' I thought: 'What is *back*, there is no going back, there is no forward, no sideways, no up, no down, only us, and we are walking.' I said: 'What do you mean by: the end?' My voice squeaked, resounding from the red infinity. 'Yes,' she said in a remote way, slightly sadistic, 'the end.' And at the same moment I came to a halt, frozen to the spot. Every bit of sense in standing there oozed away, Maria's hair became a virulent green and transformed into a formless mass of snakes, the face became drawn into that of an apathetic dead corpse. The eyes large as eggs, with deep shadows, the nose crumbled to the bone in desperation, the well-formed mouth with the pearly row of teeth now became like a massive basalt block, with purple-rotten teeth that seemed to become larger. The hands as well as the feet metamorphosed to pale-yellow polyps, five on each hand and foot, and her navel became a mirror in which all of the village could be seen . . .'

When we place the story and the drawing (see illustration) beside descriptions by Rudolf Steiner of worlds beyond the threshold (macro-microcosm) and we place beside that the images from *Parzival* of Wolfram von Eschenbach, the similarities are remarkable (the persons in question had never heard of Parzival).

First the story: it seems the farmers bar the way outward, and force the story's main characters to take the inward path (passing the inner threshold). The doors, passages, and stairways seem to depict the threshold itself. What is remarkable is the quiet, the space, and the redness. When the boy in the story has come to the conclusion that he can no longer return, Maria suddenly changes into a monstrous apparition.

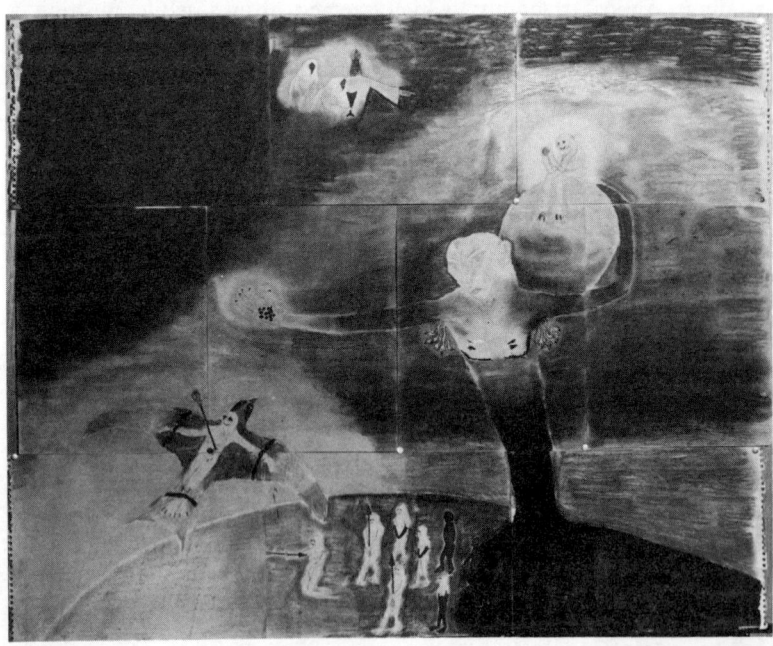

Threshold

This seems like a description of an encounter with the 'Lesser Guardian of the Threshold'. The description of Parzival's Lesser Guardian (Cundry) is identical. The navel mirror in which the village can be seen is also found in the Castle of Wonders, where a pillar inside the castle mirrors all of the outside world.

Later in the story of this boy, the monstrous apparition passes judgement on the main person: "The ideas you have are all very nice," she says ironically. In *Knowledge of Higher Worlds, and How to Attain It* Steiner describes the Lesser Guardian: "A truly terrible spectral being confronts him, . . ." and he describes further that this being is made up of all that which is imperfect in us. The monstrousness is the visible judgment of our own shortcomings. No-one can stand the view of this being without preparation. This being prevents us from going further on the path inwards.

The drawing appears more related to images from the macrocosmos (the world of the night). It appears to depict a complete path of development, with such Parzival symbols as the spear and goblet. The human being must kill his lower self – as an image of the purification – after which he is raised by the bird (a sort of kingfisher or hummingbird, which is often depicted by South-American Indians as a mythical bird). The large being tempts the bird with seeds he holds in his hand. Apparently you can pass by this gigantic being, and are then allowed to sit on the (world?) globe, holding your own (world?) globe in your hand, as a kind of state of perfection. Upon entering the macrocosm an encounter takes place with the 'Greater Guardian of the Threshold'. The large being seems a bit like that. Contrary to the story, which refers to many passages and doors, there is a sense of enormous space.

From the account of how the drawing and the story came about it is quite clear they were not thought out in advance – they happened completely unconsciously and spontaneously. Both also bear marks of inward as well as outward threshold crossings. Thus the large figure in the drawing certainly seems to have features of the Lesser Guardian as well. Because these are unconscious creations it is difficult to discern precisely where the images come from.

Now we can say: Yes, sure, but that is nothing special, that is simply fantasy and free association. True enough, in itself there is nothing special about it, but there is an important difference between the way these forms of expression came about and creating fantasy. The boys themselves did not experience this as fantasy. Everyone can write such stories, but one knows one is creating fantasy. If you were to tell one of these boys it is only a fantasy, you would hurt him deeply. He experiences something very real and profound in this story or in the drawing. We short-change the adolescent (and the spiritual world) by dismissing this as fantasy.

**What, precisely, is crossing the threshold?**

Rudolf Steiner, and Bernard Lievegoed describe the two kinds of threshold crossings. The first is the so-called crossing 'inward', into the microcosm of the physical, etheric, and astral body.* The human being of the present is protected from incarnating too far into his own bodily nature by his sense impressions, which, as it were, divert his attention. If the sense impressions were to be eliminated the consciousness could descend into the bodily nature. If one starts on this descent one crosses a threshold between the sense world and a world not perceptible to the senses. This threshold is guarded by the so-called 'Lesser Guardian of the Threshold' with whom one then has an encounter. This guardian is composed, as indicated, of all that in which we fell short in working on our own being. If the correct preparations have been carried out, it is possible to pass this Guardian without ill effects, and to descend further into the microcosm.

In the Middle Ages this was still practised as a conscious initiation by mystics, such as the Spanish mystic, Teresa de Avila. She knew the divine world, and herself, before she descended. She eliminated sense impressions as much as possible by living in a monastery, and by meditation. After her encounter with the Lesser Guardian, she only described herself as a miserable wretch. In relation to the ancient Egyptian path of initiation, Lievegoed describes how an encounter with the Lesser Guardian leads to a sense of destruction, against which the Egyptian initiation pupil was guarded by hierophants.

The other crossing of the threshold is the so-called path outward, into the macrocosm. Here one begins to be aware of being active in the realm of nature. We are protected against this, too, because we lose consciousness (in sleep) the moment we approach this threshold. We know a first beginning of this when during a sleepless night we notice movements and noises in our darkened bedroom. When we do cross this threshold, we meet the so-called 'Greater Guardian of the Threshold' who appears as the image of the perfected human being we could become. 'I am nothing, I am not worthy to appear before the countenance of God,' says Teresa de Avila after a meeting with this Guardian.

However, unlike Teresa de Avila, the youth of the present day has had no inner preparation and has no knowledge of the spiritual world. The encounter with the spiritual world, and possibly with the Guardian, takes place without preparation and unconsciously. This is not without consequences. These consequences can manifest themselves in three, and possibly more, ways:

1. One encounters a completely unfamiliar world, in which, as mentioned, totally different laws and forces prevail from those in earthly reality. Because the transitions occur spontaneously during every-day activities (such as homework, in the case of our writer), the earthly and the spiritual laws and forces get mixed up. As a result, the boy in question did not know any longer what is true and what is not. He no longer trusted what he saw, or thought he saw. He became disoriented and estranged from earthly reality. (To get a better understanding of these intermixing realities, c.f. the magic-realistic novels of Hubert Lampo.)

2. The intensity of the laws and forces in the spiritual world is much greater than that of the earth's, at least in the experience of the adolescent. It seems that more is possible, there is more tension, greater danger, a greater truth, greater happiness. The normal daily reality is boring, uninviting, and dull in comparison. This brings about a continual yearning for 'the other world'. (If one wants to understand this better, read the part of the Parzival epic dealing with the Castle of Wonders and the Grail Castle.)

3. Steiner describes how an unprepared meeting with the Lesser Guardian results in a devastating sense of shame, and that a meeting with the Greater Guardian evokes a paralysing fear. (c.f. Lievegoed's *Man on the Threshold* on the Egyptian and Nordic initiations.

## How this is related to drugs

I have often shown the drawing and the story mentioned earlier to residents of Arta. They recognize these immediately as LSD images. In other words, the threshold experiences of both boys are related to drug experiences.

We can surmise that threshold experiences are re-experienced in, at least, hashish/marijuana and LSD. Among the young people of my acquaintance who have smoked hashish, eight out of ten stop after some experimentation. Two go on. Why? Because the drug satisfies a hankering after the experience from beyond the threshold? After all, hash does result in a sense of greater intensity, and relieves boredom, as well as fear and shame. These two out of ten start to smoke hash regularly, and start experimenting with LSD, which makes the experience all the more intensive and thrilling. At the same time, regular use leads to more encounters with the Guardians, and the shame and fear are reinforced. Eventually, they gain the upper hand. Even ten joints or trips do not help (this is when the so-called bad trips begin). Of the two young people who get this far, one decides it has been enough, and stops (not without difficulty, incidentally), and the other starts to use heroin and discovers that the all-pervading shame and fear have disappeared. Heroin numbs feeling and consciousness.

If the above experience is a general one, we have to worry only about two out of ten hash-smoking youths. We will have to learn to recognize these two at an early stage. Or even better: We will have to learn to recognize young people who have *conscious* threshold experiences.

**Practical suggestions**

Above all, it is important that we take the young people in question seriously. The worst thing is to start moralizing. Even though this is a temptation, the practical consequences lead to the greatest difficulties. For to take them seriously means not to place limits. Moralizing means setting limits. And limits is what this is all about. The doubt and the fear of intervening too early or too late make it terribly difficult to do the right thing. The limitations that are imposed must be based on insight into what has been described above, and on love for the individual. That, too, is an open door, but love and understanding cease abruptly when hash gets into it. The adolescent notices the panicky reactions of adults, and that only makes it all the more exciting. And whether we like it or not, hash is there, and we live in a time when everything has to become a personal experience before it can be understood. A mere prohibition has no meaning.

Finally, what is of importance, too, is that we help the adolescent with threshold experiences to find 'anchors' in earthly reality. Those who can not distinguish what is real from what is not real can, for instance, practise intensive observation exercises. Those who by means of excitement want to banish boredom could be offered excitement in all kinds of difficult, useful tasks (repairing the roof, for instance). Those who are blocked by fear and shame can benefit from intimate, confidential conversations.

Perhaps a kind of remedial teacher or counsellor who can relieve the usual teacher in this area would be a solution. For threshold crossings with or without drugs can be expected to be only the beginning of the phenomenon: 'Man has crossed the threshold'.

* See B. C. J. Lievegoed *Man on the Threshold*, op. cit.

* See Chapter 9 and Dr Derek Blinko's account of these terms on p56 for a fuller explanation.

# Chapter 5

# Arta and its residents

*Margit Ilgen*

In the following, a brief sketch will be given of the Arta program. First, two ex-residents will talk about their lives, their addiction, and the process they went through at Arta. Since the account of the residents themselves seems to me to be the most important part, the description of the Arta program will only be an overview.

*Timmy* (age thirty, three years out of Arta, in training as a gardener, and working in that field):
  'Until I was eleven, I had a great childhood in a good family. Then we moved to Japan, and when I had recovered from the asthma I had suffered from until then, I came apart, as it were. I didn't do much work in school anymore, and I rejected family life. I got into all kinds of mischief with my friends (thefts, fights), and we started on alcohol and pills. In the first instance that was for me a way to be part of the gang, but the highs turned out to be a good way not to feel little problems, such as unrequited infatuations.
  'My parents disapproved of my behaviour, but then thought it would all blow over. Back in Holland (at age fifteen), my father insisted I go to the Athenaeum[†]. The transition was too great. I couldn't keep up, and didn't feel there was any reason why I should. I smoked joints all day with my friends, and didn't observe any rules. Contact with my mother remained reasonably good. My father worked in another city, and when he'd come home I'd have an attitude of 'who do you think you are that you can push me around?' Besides grass, I also started doing LSD.
  'At 17 I left school when I had to repeat the fourth year for the second time. My girl friends dropped me, and my parents got a divorce. I stayed with my father, whom I couldn't talk to at all. Outwardly I kept pretty cool, but inwardly I did not really cope with all this. But then I also started using amphetamines, which made my inner chaos complete. Because I had a job, I lost touch with my school friends who had stayed at school. I couldn't accept that, had the feeling I had failed. One day I

flipped on LSD, and decided to give it up, as well as amphetamines, but after two months I was addicted to heroin. From them on (at age twenty) until I was twenty-eight I was just one pile of misery, all related to the fact that I saw no purpose in life. Often I stopped taking (the drug), but then quickly gave in again, for there was only a big hole full of misery piled upon misery. I didn't know how I could get over it, and why. Tried not to get in deeper, waiting for something to happen that would enable me to get over it.

'At twenty-five I realized I shouldn't keep waiting, but should do something myself. After eight withdrawal programs, which I quit every time, I got myself admitted to a psychiatric clinic just to get off the street. A year and a half later I left there with a negative report, and within three months I was addicted again.

'I woke up in the police station (arrested for stealing). I realized I still had a choice while later I might get years in the pen. Through my mother I heard about Arta. What I liked there was the quietness and the rhythm. There was a time for talking and for working, for therapy and for sleep. Because of the absence of compulsion and punishment I could grow, and show who I was in my own good time and the way I wanted. The possibilities I had as a human being were addressed, and I felt stimulated to unfold them. For the first time I found examples in other people, instead of therapists who did not want to deal with me as a human being because I was a junkie. Personal guidance was no longer a dirty word, and not everything had to be done in groups. I learned to trust one person, with whom I could share my problems. The programs I had done before were all aimed at taking the illness away (the addiction) and then adapting to the outside world. I'd always had the feeling that that didn't make sense. At Arta I experienced that behind that outside world there also has to be an inner one, just as I have an inner life. That is how I could feel a connection with things again. Certain ideas appealed to me, for instance that nothing happens without cause. You are not a bad-luck Charlie for nothing. That is how I got out of that negative world and was encouraged once more to deal with life positively and actively.

'The most important thing was that I started to see again that things were worthwhile. I had something to aim for again – at first in only small ways, but that went together with a process of feeling good about life again, experiencing a connection again with what I felt and did. With small daily tasks, and by means of hobbies I never had before, I can now get out of these negative moods.

'Because of the celebration of the season's festivals I came to realize that there is a rhythm in me, and one in nature, with a connection between the two. What I feel at a certain time of the year is not only my problem. This gives a kind of peace.

'When I left Arta I felt I was normal. I didn't want anything else. I discovered life outside Arta was not as different as I had feared at the beginning of the fourth phase. It was for me a continuing path.

'The feeling of getting away from it all for a while that dope can give is still tempting, but it is no longer an alternative for me.'

*Sandra* (age twenty-nine, four years out of Arta, working in a curative institute and training as a curative teacher):

'I had a good childhood, in a warm home, with fine parents (in Australia). When I was ten, and near death from an attack of jaundice, I saw a lot of things. From then on I knew that there was something else besides the life that is visible, and I started looking for this. First I experimented with seances and hypnosis, and later, when we had moved to Holland, (age fourteen) I thought I would find it with some hippie friends who smoked dope, among other things. I hung around with that group and from weed and hash I moved to LSD, speed, and cocaine. When I took those things I saw images I had also experienced when I was ill.

'I was always looking for confirmation that there was something else, and felt a resistance against the world that didn't see this. I couldn't understand what the sense of all these people's lives could be without this something else.

'My father had a pretty good idea what I was up to, my mother thought it wasn't anything serious. But I evaded them, and despite all warnings this search for that other world was too strong in me to realize that what I was doing was harmful.

'When I was 16, my father died, and at seventeen I was solidly addicted to heroin. I was living in a sort of dream state, like a plant, and lost all contact with my environment. I was dismissed from school, which didn't bother me, for I'd had just to accept what they spoon-fed me there, and I had received no answers to my questions.

'At twenty-one I realized something was wrong, tried to kick my habit and return to school. But I came into this void, which the world was for me, and became addicted again (age twenty-three).

'In prison (three months for theft) I woke up, as it were. From my social worker I got a brochure about Arta, and what it said about thinking, feeling and willing appealed to me.

'While I wrote my biography for the introductory interview, I saw how I had always resisted the world, and for the first time asked myself: What am I going to do about it?

'In the beginning, in Arta, I found it very difficult to place the responsibility for myself in the hands of others. Often I thought of the co-workers: Is that how they are supposed to set an example for us? But I stayed because I sensed something that was good in the intention out of which they worked. Through the bond that grew between me and those who helped me, I got through that first period. This was a time in which I had a lot to sort out; the hurt and the grief that had been erased through dope resurfaced. Also many questions arose about what had happened in my life thus far. Often I was shocked when confronted with aspects of myself that I had vaguely known about, but never consciously acknowledged. Certain views I got during the work at Arta are still of use to me.

'I learned to look at myself, discovered that you could develop yourself, and that this was meaningful. Although I sometimes became discouraged by the confrontations with my shortcomings, particularly in the third and fourth phase, I nevertheless knew there was no turning back. Actually, I had already made that choice while in prison, although at the time I didn't know where to look for the motivation. This I found at Arta. Here I became aware that the earth is permeated by something spiritual, which is how I could connect to it. I felt that with my own development I was responsible for other human beings and the earth, as if I had to make good the dark experiences I had had, among others in hypnosis and seances. In the lectures on evolution I received answers to questions I had long had, and when there were lectures about religion as well, I thought, well, at least they are not dogmatic!

'Saying good-bye to Arta was like leaving home, although in the fourth phase I was at first very unsure. When it was time to take my leave, I was confident that it had to be possible now. I did have the feeling that with many things I'd never stop learning. Sometimes the dope experiences return, as if suddenly I feel a flash, as with a shot. Momentarily that is tempting, but in that same moment I see the consequences in a flash, and then I don't want it anymore.'

In each phase of life, man has to develop certain inward and outward qualities, which enable him to unfold in the world. If, for reasons either within himself or in the environment, he does not take up this development, he will lack the instruments to go on. This lack leads to feelings of impotence, of being out of sorts, and rejection of life, which may lead to drug use. In turn, addiction to drugs puts a total stop to development, and leads to isolation and indifference with respect to one's own development.

On the basis of these ideas, and the experience with the residents, Arta has developed a phased program in which residents have the opportunity to 'repeat' certain phases of life, as it were. Thus they can gather up again the 'instruments' that will enable them to go their own way. In addition, through its community structure, Arta invites the residents to show an interest in their own development, in other people, and in the world. That is why Arta is not only a 'therapeutic' community, but also a living and working community.

The first phase of the program takes place on a small farm. What counts particularly in this first 'Arta phase', just as in the first seven years of the child, is to rebuild a healthy body by means of a rhythmic life style, which is regulated in a protected environment. Through the care shown by the co-workers for the residents, something in the way of trust in other people can arise again, while the vegetable garden and the animals on the farm ask for the residents' care, and through this they establish a connection with them.

After about seven weeks, the residents go to the Witte Hull (the main residence) in Zeist for the start of the second phase. A rhythmic and sheltered life style, among others through house rules that separate residents from the drug scene, remain the same in this phase and the next. Gradually, the residents must transform this life rhythm of the environment into a routine of their own. Now that physical withdrawal is behind them, the emotional life, previously dimmed by drugs, comes to life again. By means of fairy-tales, worked through artistically and also through drama, music, and group eurythmy, this inner world is, as it were, nourished. In personal conversations and group discussions residents have the opportunity to talk about their lives, share their experiences, and work this out to some extent. Daily chores in the house, the garden, and the weaving and woodworking shops demand that residents really wake up to the here and now.

In the life phase from seven to fourteen, the child develops a routine of its own, guided by the parents, and also a life of feeling that is still fairy-tale-like and nourished by stories, games, songs, etc. This forms the basis for healthy life processes and a rich soul life at a later age. In the second phase of the Arta program, these elements return.

At about twelve or thirteen, the growing child often becomes painfully aware of his own being and of the reality of the outside world. The fantasies and fairy-tales of childhood are no longer valid. The child has become 'earth-ripe'. Searching for his own judgments, which initially still swing back and forth between passionate sympathies and antipathies, the child, in puberty, attempts to establish the relation between himself and the world as it is. In this life phase judgments based on feelings of pleasure and displeasure have to grow into real interests, on which later on an adult relationship to fellow human beings and the world can be based. Education based on the authority of parents and teachers has to give way gradually to a search for self-knowledge, ideals, and responsibility based on mutual friendship.

This phase of life returns in the third phase of the Arta program. Each resident now gets a permanent advisor with whom he or she has weekly conversations and who 'accompanies' him or her to the end of the program.

Group therapy is complemented by individual therapy, aimed at the personal problems of the resident. Fairy-tales and stories give way to a study program that encourages self-motivation, and demands judgments and an interest in the world. In work and daily life the residents take on responsibilities of their own, in which they test their own abilities within the community. Along with these responsibilities, the residents gradually gain more personal freedom.

Most of the residents started on drugs at the beginning of puberty, in search for something else other than the hard reality of the world, and/or because of an inability to take responsibility for their own future in this world. With respect to the latter, the 'choice' is repeated in the third phase of the Arta program when the residents have the experience that the dream world of drug addiction is definitely behind them, and they have come face to face with a still indistinct future, fully conscious of themselves (and their own problems).

In the fourth phase of the Arta program, the residents have a number of work- and training placements outside the community, which they have selected in consultation with their advisors and an aftercare co-worker. Now they also have the freedom to leave the premises unescorted, and to manage their own money. In the fourth phase they evaluate their experiences on a weekly basis with the aftercare co-worker.

In the second phase, the residents had told each other about their biographies. In the third phase they had gone more deeply into the important aspects of the biography with their adviser. In the fourth phase they are given a biography workshop, in which the objective laws of the course of human life are dealt with. This allows the residents to see their own experiences in the larger context.

A genuine sharing of responsibility for the atmosphere in the group, for taking in younger residents, and for the practicalities of every-day life is demanded of the fourth-phase resident.

Just as at around nineteen the young person leaves school and the parental home in order to find his way in the outside world, so in this phase at Arta the objective is to disconnect from the Arta community. In contact with the real outside world, the resident now has the opportunity to practise with what he or she has thus far gained, while simultaneously his sense of responsibility is challenged at home. In this process, by trial and error, he finds tentative answers to such questions as: Who am I, what do I want, what can I do? Gradually, development through the environment gives way to self-development ('Arta' is an old Swedish word for 'self-development').

By this time the resident has been at Arta for about a year. Although the transitions from one phase to the next depend on the individual developmental process of each resident, the second, third and fourth phase each take about three months on average.

From the experiences of the fourth phase a picture of the future emerges gradually, as well as the need for independence to take one's own life in hand again. When this has taken on a more concrete form, in finding living accommodation, a job, and/or training, the resident usually has the experience that it is now time to go to work: 'Because now it is really the beginning.'

This program should not be seen as a fixed method for solving the problem of drug addiction. Each resident has his or her own way of developing in it and experiencing it. The program of phases should rather be looked upon as a framework that has proven to be meaningful in practice, and provides residents and co-workers with guidelines for their activities. The question of meaning in life, from which can grow the real motivation to kick the habit is not answerable by a method. The source for the work at Arta, and the impulse from which Arta derives its form and content lie in Anthroposophy.

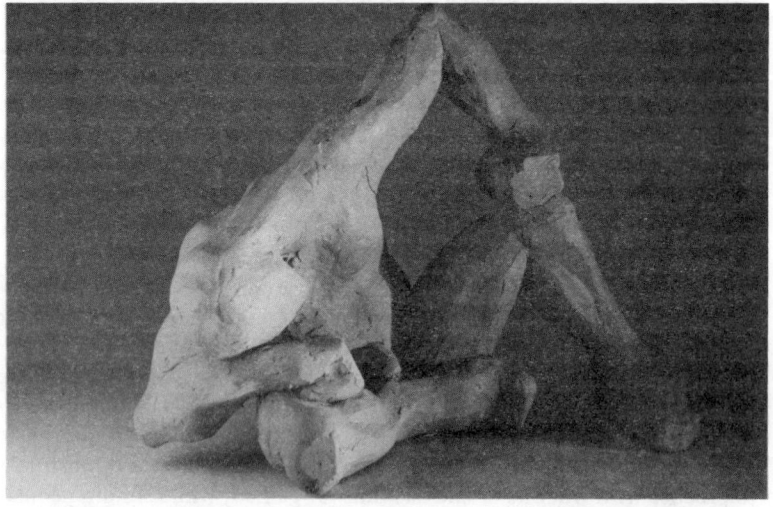

... "depression" ...

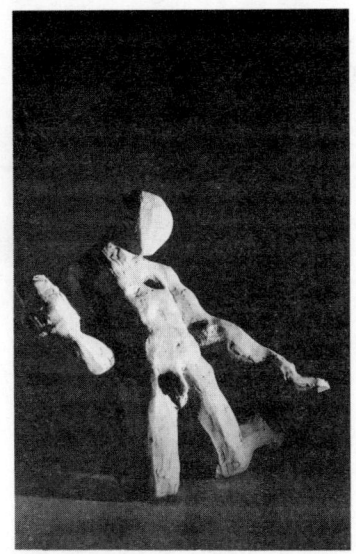

. . . "emptyness . . . a question" . . .

. . . "intellect only . . . rationalizing" . . .

. . . "only feeling" . . .

. . . "balance between intellect and feeling" . . .

With many thanks to Timmy and Sandra.

† A high school programme focussed on the classics and languages

# Chapter 6

# Addiction from the point of view of parents

Conversations recorded by *Peter Scheers*

*The mother*

At a certain moment my daughter called and wanted to talk to me. Mom, I am on hard drugs, you know, but I want to get off them. The fear that rose in me – about that child living in such a tension, and having to get out of it one way or another. I'd had some inkling she was using drugs, many times she would be sitting there, and we would say, what is the matter with you, but she would never answer that clearly. The whole idea became such an obsession with me that it was the only thing I could discuss with my friends when they came to visit. Talk, talk, talk.

But meanwhile I realized she was also calling for help from my husband and me, and particularly from me. You think you did everything right, and now it became clear that things had not gone well at all.

At home she had probably missed a part of the bringing-up process. I mean, for instance the preparation for the season's festivals – the idea of celebrating the festivals in a spiritual way instead of the tradition of merely exchanging gifts that we were brought up with.

Because of our work we were always so busy outside with all kinds of things. It was all thinking and willing. What goes in between was often missing. In my opinion, this is what she must have sensed unconsciously: something is missing, there has to be something else. From school reports it is clear that she really enjoyed the artistic subjects and periods that are given in such a creative way at the Waldorf School. But school itself, the fact she had to go, that she'd been resisting. Perhaps we started in the Waldorf school too late – only in Class Eight (at thirteen years old).

To be fair, I should add that not every child – who hasn't gone to a Waldorf School, or has suffered from a superficial upbringing at home, will necessarily get on drugs.

The child's constitution, aptitude, temperament, etc., also play a significant role in how a person develops his/her biography. I could mention very striking aspects with regard to my daughter, but that is not the subject of this conversation.

Because of the tensions in connection with my daughter's drug use, I was forced into the role of guardian, which made me realize: I have to do something myself, about myself.

You can't ask of your child to do inner work and act as if there is nothing the matter with yourself.

Via the anthroposophical society I got into several courses and lectures. One course prompted me to start studying fairy-tales and their background.

With coloured wood we started making the characters out of fairy-tales, and through the care and love we put into the making of them developed another connection. The contact with others, by working on something like this together, was a revelation for me. It is difficult to explain it in words, but it gave me courage and strength to deal with the problems that presented themselves in connection with my daughter.

I more or less found myself again, and from that was able to concern myself more with spiritual science. You can't concentrate on that when you are restless and agitated, and can't sleep at night.

I was particularly touched by some lectures dealing with human development, religion, and the theme of love in connection with health and sickness. I made notes of everything.

Because of everything that happened I came to realize how superficially I had worked on self-development, which is then also lacking in the way you bring up your children. And I don't mean only the spiritual aspect, but also a relationship based on trust and love. Things were always merely emotional – reacting to each other without really listening to each other.

We cried together in the kitchen, but to really show all it did to me, no. I didn't really want to impose on her, and my daughter was at that time inaccessible anyway because of drug use. She wasn't herself. She was a different person. She did sense it when we saw each other, but it was never expressed. What I did was to vent it on my husband and other children. I had to get rid of some of my fear and grief.

Now that I have been dealing with this in a different way lately, I wonder whether it couldn't have been like this much earlier. But you know how it is, I had so much to do, the house, the kids, and some evenings my husband and I liked to go out once in a while too, even though he was often away for work at night.

But now I can experience so much more...

## The father

I didn't exactly panic when I was confronted with the fact that one of my children was on hard drugs. That's the difference between my wife and I in how we coped with it. When confronted with problems, I meet them as in a game of chess, strongly analytical. In the first instance I considered the structure of my daughter's character, and, rightly or wrongly, I did not find any reason for blaming myself.

At that moment I could only react the way my parents dealt with me. They left me completely free, and I hardly confided in them about the things that occupied me most. That is how I got the strong feeling: You have to manage as much as possible on your own. And then you expect this of your children too.

There have been great differences in the connections I had with each of my children. We did a lot of things together, but you do experience each child in a different way.

In particular later on I became aware that with this girl I had much less the experience of togetherness than with the other kids. She was by nature more independent anyway, and when later the problems came she withdrew even more fundamentally.

She strongly resisted everything I would tell her on different occasions. In retrospect, she resisted my aloof attitude in this, as if I were an outsider who her problem didn't concern. It was partly also protection, which I needed. I had also to cope with what was happening to my daughter and the worry about what would become of her – that worried me a lot.

That was perhaps an excuse again, consciously or unconsciously, for my own inability really to do something for her. That's why I was hoping that she could go somewhere else for her drug problem. In talking with my wife, and with others, it has become clear to me that in the interaction with the children the life of feeling had not always been nourished, besides what my wife had already mentioned with respect to giving a more spiritual content to the children's upbringing.

When the Waldorf School I attended was closed during the war, my mother arranged to have me participate in conversation groups in which we spoke about the most fundamental aspects of life. I got a lot out of these. Talking about things made you think.

Well, something like that was lacking for our children. They always managed in their own way, but I could have played a greater part in helping them to deepen it.

The war on drugs in which we have become involved at the present time makes you stop to think, as a parent, and particularly when it concerns one of your own children. Has my life changed fundamentally because of this? Not to the same extent as this has been the case for my wife. I need a little bit longer.

My connections with others, and specifically the children, was always strongly influenced by thinking – it had to be functional, analytical – with little from the heart.

In that respect something did happen to me.

# Chapter 7

# Aftercare: A social remedy . . . or remedy for society?

*Aalt van den Berg*

About fifty people are involved in aftercare at Arta – ex-residents, co-workers, entrepreneurs, and volunteers. They looked after the businesses that have been started by Arta, and the training placements and residential and study groups (the next article, by Sjon van Schaick, includes a brief summary of these).

I will concern myself more with the way in which the people involved work together in dealing with the problems arising in aftercare.

**The origin – an exciting process**

When as co-workers we had decided to start with aftercare, we hardly knew how to approach this task. We knew very little about it, and had no idea where to start. We could not wait for something just to happen – the situation did not allow this – so we decided to take a step into the unknown.

Things became clearer through what came into being. Gradually, shops, machinery, living accommodation, and meeting rooms began to appear. Simultaneously we gained some insights, motives and objectives became clearer, and we began to work on a form of organization.

The starting point was the sort of questions that in one way or another live in the ex-residents of Witte Hull in their encounters with society. The ex-residents play an active role in the development of aftercare activities. Co-workers, directors, the authorities, and society as a whole all play a role. Together they constitute a complex of forces that is hard to describe.

The form that aftercare will eventually take depends on the creative abilities of all those concerned.

It is an exciting process – exciting in the sense that it is a challenge, but also literally. There are tensions resulting from the fact that time and again you get stuck, you grope in the dark, and you are thrown back on yourself. But if you can stand this tension, if you can handle it, the possibility arises in you to let something else come to the fore. You can then resist the temptation to run away that arises in you at such times, which ultimately can lead to addiction.

**Facing hidden questions**

A resident leaving our community is comparable to a child who has reached adulthood and leaves home. The family is a community within society with a quality all of its own, which expresses itself in the family culture, agreements, rules and tasks. An important pedagogical influence is the extent to which family life can be an example to the growing child. Gradually, however, protest against this example increases. Just as a physical heredity is transformed into an individual identity, the individual also wants to transform this social example called family into an expression of himself.

The way this loosening process takes its course is different in individual cases, and can teach us quite a lot, whether we are the one to leave, or the one to remain behind.

What happiness there is when you realize you can have confidence in the path the other has chosen, out of his own insights, norms, and values! What support you receive from this confidence when it is given to you!

This kind of leave-taking takes place regularly at the Hull. There are people who, after leaving, can steer a pretty straight course on their own. But what raises many questions is that the majority indicate they can not quite go it alone in society.

Has the preparation been insufficient? Were they too sheltered? Was there too little space for development, or a lack of insight?

Or should you look at it from the other side? Is it perhaps that they really lack sufficient strength and will need help in any case?

One can also look for the cause of this difficulty in society. Is it unhealthy, hardened?

It is typical that our ex-residents in such cases could not indicate where their feelings of insecurity came from, nor could they articulate how we might still be able to do something for them. For the co-workers, too, this continued to be puzzling. At such a time there is temptation to call it quits and close the door. The program in the therapeutic community has been completed; now, a stiff upper lip, and take care of yourself! But these are people who go beyond what is rational. They go all the way!

It became clear to us that the connection must not be severed. The door had to remain open, even if what they are doing is totally incomprehensible to us.

We co-workers decided to start sharing in their lives. From guiding to sharing their lives demands a change in attitude, of the co-workers as well as of the ex-residents. Basic to this decision was the agreement that, whatever happens, you always remain accessible for each other. This agreement demands continuous interest in, acceptance of, and understanding for each other.

This means meeting social reality together, exchanging experiences of the inner and outer world. It means a man-to-man relationship based on equality, in which both can grow. In meeting the experiential world of the other, the situation itself often makes clear what has to be done.

**The experiential world**

What is it that lives in the souls of young people? What makes their soul world so fearful, chaotic, insecure, and, sometimes, aggressive? Of course I can only speak in generalities here, based on the experience with the people that come to us. I will highlight only one aspect, for I believe this to be characteristic for many of our residents: Many of them are bothered by the sense of alienation from the surrounding world. It is apparent that the relationship with the outside world is a difficult one. Often there is a clear 'NO' in reaction to what is observed and experienced in the outside world.

The difficulty here is that no alternative presents itself. Then the situation quickly becomes dangerous, for when it continually closes itself off, the soul loses its grip on reality. Wretchedness, meaninglessness, and aimlessness are the result, and heavy depression can gain the upper hand. This process is depicted beautifully in the fairy-tale of the Sleeping Beauty, in which the soul becomes shut off from the thorny outside world.

Gradually development gets stuck, which increases the chance that one will seek an escape route, for instance in drugs. The addiction to drugs, ultimately, ensures that one will become stuck in all aspects of life.

Addiction goes hand in hand with a stagnation of development. I believe that, potentially, anyone can become addicted.

The addiction is not determined by the means, although there are substances that are more strongly addictive than others. What counts is the effect the substance has on our organism, how it changes the experiences of the soul. Snacking, watching TV, doing sports, etc., can all become means of addiction because of the way we handle these things. To make it conscious that one deliberately seeks to attain a desired effect can lead to an acknowledgement of addiction, and that is the first step towards recovery.

But what is it that has to take the place of the escape route in such a way that life seems worth living again? This question leads to an investigation of the hindrances in which the soul became stuck. These hindrances can come from the outside world, for instance repression, a one-sided education, or a lack of cultural example.

The hindrances can also lie in the soul itself, there where the soul is able to uncover and experience beauty, goodness, and truth in the outside world.

Here I would like to discuss an aspect that arises from still another side. There is an unpredictable factor amidst the ordinary life of the soul. The soul becomes aware of certain tendencies – mostly vague and semiconscious, but of a special character. It is as if another world announces itself, but from the depths of the soul.

It is a vague world because the conceptual life can not quite grasp it. On the other hand, our experience of it tells us that a reality exists here, which is intimate in character, and unimaginably essential.

The awakening of this world might be the reason why the relationship with the outer world seems to deteriorate. In that case the cause of the difficulties must be sought not only in the past, but in that which seeks to manifest itself.

Something unknown, something that can become clear only in the future is in this case the cause of the experience of confusion that can arouse such fear and uncertainty.

Then it is the soul's task to gain an understanding for the reality that makes itself felt in one's inner world, as well as for the reality of the outside world.

The individual faces the task of bringing the outer world into agreement with that other world, which is spiritual in nature. This may start at the very beginning of puberty. The shaping of the personality must then take place in relation to those two worlds. It is clear that this is not a process that is completed at age twenty one, but continues during the further course of life.

This process manifests itself in the sort of questions one continually asks oneself, such as: who am I, really? where did I come from? and is what I want in fact the right thing to do?

**A path between adaptation and isolation**

The spiritual tendencies that gradually awaken in the soul were characterized by Maria Röschl-Lehrs as *'The Second Man Within Us'*.

This is the title of a book she wrote on this theme from her experience as leader of the Youth Section at the Goetheanum.[†] The question, who is this 'second man' within us, is answered by Rudolf Steiner: it is something that lived in a previous incarnation and in the present enters life in a shadowy manner. Because of the awakening of this second 'man' we become, in our experience, citizens of two worlds.

Within the therapeutic community a culture has arisen that tries to take the presence of this 'second man' into account. But this aspect also has to be absorbed into the cultural life, to ray out from there into society as a whole.

Arta wants to make a contribution to this by broadening its scope from that of merely a therapeutic community to one that encompasses social life in general.

It is heartening to meet people everywhere, and particularly in the anthroposophical movement and society, who are striving in the same direction. But elsewhere, too, it is becoming apparent that people want to express this 'second man'.

Think of the student riots of the Sixties. The rioters wanted to go beyond the intellectual approach to the sense-perceptible world. In movements such as the peace movement and that of the environmentalists there are people who are not prepared to submit to the existing system of justice because they experience fundamental injustice.

Within the Me-Mo movement and its volunteer workers, are people who have discovered non-material motives within themselves, which become the driving force for their actions. (Me-Mo is a network of small enterprises inspired by E.F. Schumacher's ideas.)

Thus a network can grow. In this network one can meet something in the outer world that has a relation to what lives in one's own inner world. It is of great importance to the youth of today in general that this should, indeed, happen. But there are also forces that will do everything within their power to prevent people from becoming citizens of two worlds. One of these forces ultimately aims for total adaptation to the sense world. The other leads to isolation, and a sense of being misunderstood within one's own inner world or institution, threatened by the big bad world outside.

You need fellow human beings on the path that runs between these two forces. On your own you get caught time and again.

In aftercare an attempt is made to form a community, a network, in which the individual is central. From this the encounter and co-operation with others can arise.

The term 'aftercare' is misleading, and does not reflect what is really meant. The facilities that come into being are designated as 'arrangements for social rehabilitation for ex-residents, but also as an arrangement in which people can work for the rehabilitation of society, then the objective of co-workers, volunteers, and ex-residents is properly understood.

* The Goetheanum, Dornach, Switzerland is the centre of the Anthroposophical Society, and the Youth Section of the Society works with young people's questions.

# Chapter 8

# Aftercare facilities

*Sjon van Schaick*

The following describes something of what ex-residents and co-workers have accomplished so far:

In the first place, more than five years ago (1980) a restaurant, *Lembas*, was started up in Driebergen. It was followed by a woodworking shop, and later by a candle-making and pottery shop. These enterprises are run by ex-residents and volunteers. Arta made it possible for them to get started, and still provides support. The objective is to experience the reality of economic life, but in such a way that 'the second man' in us gets a chance for expression. This means that these enterprises aim for a social climate in which each person can serve the economic goal with his/her own capacities. After much experimentation it appears that within these businesses three conditions emerge under which this social climate, and, therefore, the individual employee, can thrive. These are:
1) The businesses have to be small enough so that all workers know each other personally;
2) The entire productive process has to be understandable for all employees, from basic raw material to the customer;
3) All employees must have the opportunity to share in innovation, both with respect to the product, and to the business as a whole.

With these three conditions, it seems, a beginning has been made tentatively with a new way of working that seems to attract many young people, including, therefore, ex-residents.
 In the second place, it is now two and a half years ago (1983) since the Foundation of Promotion of Social Living Accommodation *(Stichting tot bevordering van sociale huisvesting, SBSH)* was formed. In the first instance this was a direct response to ex-residents who, after Arta, no longer wanted to live on their own in a room somewhere, or in a boarding house. The Foundation, therefore, seeks to acquire residential units in which residential communities can be formed. It now manages three

such units, for a total of twenty residents. Here, too, it seems a form has been found that can meet a much wider need than that of only ex-residents of Arta. The demand is well beyond what the Foundation can offer. To live in a community of individuals appears, on the one had, to be an answer to the problem of the isolation of a rented room, and, on the other hand, to the problem of having to adapt to the old (family) connections. In these communities it appears to be possible that each, with his own peculiarities, has enough space, while an excess of peculiarities can be absorbed, and corrected, by the other residents. In this way a climate comes about, although a fragile one, in which the 'second man in us' can be seen, regardless of whether this involves ex-residents of Arta or not. In any case, it seems that what meets the needs of ex-residents is something that has possibilities as a way of living for the future.

Finally, something about the area that is most difficult to come to grips with: education. Ex-residents of Arta want to continue to pursue the sorts of interests that have been kindled at Arta. The possibilities for doing so, however, appear to be quite scarce. On the one hand, there are often prerequisites that ex-Artans can not meet, and, on the other hand, many courses have no relevance to their experience. Moreover, too high a demand is often made on the ability to work independently, and on verbal and writing skills. All of this indicates what is really needed. Experience shows that when these needs are met it is perfectly possible to offer high-calibre courses that correspond to existing interests. The first such course was organized jointly with the Free College (Vrije Hogeschool) at Driebergen, Holland and a second one has since been started.

# Chapter 9

# What are drugs, how do they work, and what are the effects of their use?†

*Ron Dunselman*

All drugs are poisons. They affect the human sheaths by loosening the connections between them, with the result that all sorts of changes take place in human consciousness. This is what many users are after – this is why they use drugs!

These changes of consciousness are different for different drugs. I will attempt to describe the specific effects of the different drugs. Considerable space will be given to a description of the effects of LSD. In connection with this drug a number of phenomena are clearly visible that are not so clear in the case of other drugs. This is why the section on, for instance, marijuana-hashish can not be understood without reading what follows about LSD.

## LSD

LSD is made synthetically from *ergot*, a fungus that grows on rye. This fungus prevents rye from flowering normally and forming its kernels. It is a parasitic plant, which sterilizes and weakens the rye stalk for the benefit of its own propagation. It disperses in numerous spores exactly there where the rye stalk ought to flower and takes on its most rarified physical form. It thrives at the very place where the processes of dematerialization take place, but for this it relies parasitically on the rye plant, which ultimately is destroyed.

Ergot is quite toxic. When it ends up in rye bread it may cause severe poisoning symptoms, such as festering sores, burns, gangrene, and even insanity. In the Middle Ages this affliction was known as Anthony's Fire. Treatment took place in monasteries, among other things with the help of the panels painted by Matthias Grünewald for the altar of Isenheim. Ergot is, therefore, a strong poison, and so is LSD, which is made from ergot by the addition of a di-methylamide group. It can be taken only in very small amounts; 0.00003 gram is sufficient to cause a strong reaction. It causes hallucination, fantastic visions, intense colour experiences, memories from long ago, changed perceptions of space and time, and religious and mystical experiences. It may also cause threatening and terrifying visions ('flipping').

As Dr. W.A. Hoffman, who first synthesized LSD, described:
'I lost all sense of time . . . Space and time became increasingly confusing, and I became afraid that I would go insane. The worst of it was that I was fully conscious of my condition, but I could not stop it. At times I felt as if I was outside my own body. I thought I had died. My "ego" floated in space somewhere, and I saw my body lying dead on the couch.'

What actually does happen when we take a sufficiently strong poison? We die!
Dying means that the life forces (our life body or ether body) leave the physical body. Only the physical body remains on earth, as a corpse. When we take the poison LSD, a partial death takes place. We die only a little bit. A 'gap' is forced between our physical body and our ether body. When we do actually die, we observe our past life as a panorama of images spread out before us, which can be viewed all at once in its entirety. People who have been near death can recount this experience. Their etheric body was loosened from their physical body – because of a severe shock, for instance. The ether forces that became free in this manner entered consciousness (astral body), and the memories contained in these ether forces became visible.

When LSD is taken this partial death of the user can cause all kinds of long-forgotten memories to re-emerge as mental images. Often these are of an emotional nature because LSD particularly affects the liver and the kidneys. Tests with radio-actively labelled LSD have shown that LSD ends up particularly in these organs. This is where the user is most severely poisoned. This means that etheric forces that normally penetrate and build up these organs now leave them and start to affect consciousness. Since the liver is the basis for our emotional life, long-forgotten, suppressed memories of an emotional nature, which have 'weighed' on the liver and can cause lengthy periods of depression, now enter consciousness, and are re-experienced. This is why LSD has been used in the treatment of people suffering from 'concentration camp syndrome'. By means of LSD, repressed experiences of former prisoners in concentration camps were raised into consciousness, making subsequent psychotherapy possible (whether this is a desirable procedure is another question).

Another effect of LSD use is that sense perception, particularly visual perception is strongly enhanced. This, too, can be understood in the following way (1): Because of the LSD, the etheric body is detached from the physical body, particularly in the liver and kidneys, which are metabolic organs. The etheric body, however, is much more dynamic and mobile that the physical body. It has a tendency to make local processes take place elsewhere in the organism as well. Certain metabolic processes also occur in the senses, and here, too, a partial detachment of the etheric body from the physical body can take place. These detached life forces then enter consciousness and cause intense colour and light experiences. This is a process similar to what we experience when we look at a red dot on white paper for one minute. When subsequently we shift our gaze, we see a green dot on the white paper. By looking at the red dot for one minute, an intense break-down process occurs in the retina. The etheric body restores this, and we perceive these etheric forces as the after-image of red, which is green (the complementary colour of red). We observe etheric forces, therefore, for the green dot does not exist physically on the white paper.

In the same way as this after-image is caused by the impression of the etheric forces in our consciousness, intense colour and light hallucinations arise in our astral body as a result of the sensory etheric forces released through LSD.

Ether forces are released, therefore. Where do they tend to go? Back to their home, which is the cosmos! (1) We know how the plant absorbs etheric forces from the cosmos, which make the plant grow and propagate. In the human being these etheric forces are individualized in the etheric body, but as soon as they are released, they tend to float away from us, away from the earth into space. On this voyage, this trip, they take along the astral body and ego of the user, who goes out of himself into ecstasy, into a world without gravity and filled with light. 'Suddenly there was a shining light ... and the glittering beauty of Unity. All was permeated by this light – white light of incredible clarity. I felt how I flew away into the All, without weight, free from bondage, free to bathe in the blissful shine of celestial phenomena'. (John Cashman *LSD, the Miracle Drug*).

A mountain climber who survived a fall from a rock face in the Swiss alps, relates a similar experience during his fall: 'By and by I was surrounded by a wonderful blue sky with pink and pale violet clouds. Painlessly and tenderly I floated heavenwards.' (1)

In summary we can say: LSD causes a partial death because it brings about a separation of etheric and physical body. The LSD user forces a gap between his physical and ether bodies and dies partially, which explains the interest many LSD users have in the ancient Tibetan or Egyptian Books of the Dead, which may be used as preparation and as a 'manual' for 'trips'.

The question is, can the LSD user trust his experiences? Are these a source of supersensible experiences, as so many users believe? In order to answer this question, we have to consider the following: Our physical body, which occupies a certain amount of physical space, is our space body. Our etheric body, which penetrates the physical body, looks after all processes of growth, reproduction, formation regeneration – i.e., all life processes, which are a function of time. Our etheric body is our time organism. If we want to have a healthy and accurate sense of space and time, it is necessary for our physical body to be penetrated thoroughly by our ether body – they have to match. By LSD use, we force a gap between the two, with the result that the healthy sense of space and time disappears. A backyard can look like a park, or a quarter of an hour seem like a whole day.

But there is more to it still: 'In order for the human "I" and astral body not only to be filled with joy and sorrow, but consciously to be aware of these emotions, it is necessary for the astral body to be connected with the physical and etheric bodies' (Rudolf Steiner, *Occult Science – An Outline*).

The conscious awareness is there. But the contents of the LSD user's astral body (these contents derive from the partially loosened ether body) are now related to physical and etheric bodies that do not fit together, with the result that the images can not be related to correct dimensions of time and space. The physical and the etheric bodies mirror the images of the astral body in a confused way relative to spatial dimensions and time duration. They act as a distorting mirror. The world the LSD user experiences is, therefore, unreliable. Because of the partial loosening of the ether body from the physical body, the user observes himself and the world via a mirror that is partially a confusing distorting mirror, on which he can not depend at all. LSD use is, therefore, not a trustworthy source for knowledge, either with respect to the user himself (with his own emotions and memories) or to the world or the cosmos.

The same goes for other hallucinogens, such as mescaline and psylocibine.

LSD, therefore, among other things causes the user to float away from the earth, and lets him dissolve in the 'All', lets him do what ergot does – a dissolving process. But just in the way that ergot kills the rye on which it settles by preventing its further development and procreation so LSD submerges its user in real dying processes, which prevent his or her further development. Particularly with respect to the effects (not the cause), therapy must, therefore, have the aim of closing the gaps between physical and etheric body, i.e., of re-permeating the dying physical body with the ether body, re-establishing the experience of space and time. That means going towards the earth.

The basic phenomenon, therefore, is that by drug use gaps are opened between the human sheaths. With LSD, this gap falls between the physical body and the etheric body. How is it with other drugs?

## Speed

With the use of *speed* as well (i.e. chemical stimulants such as amphetamines, pervitine, etc.) a gap is forced between the physical body and the etheric body. These poisons end up in the metabolic organs and release etheric forces that, subsequently, become available to the limbs and the process of thinking. They stimulate the limbs to greater activity, which is why they are so popular with athletes. But the brain, too, is activated. One thinks faster. Fatigue and depression vanish: one can do anything.

This takes place, however, at the expense of the physical constitution, for the etheric body quickly 'burns out', depleting and exhausting one's own etheric reserves. The result is physical exhaustion and deep apathy following use of the drug. The abundantly and compulsively available metabolic-ether forces (forces of will) are reduced to zero afterwards. One has ruined one's life of volition. 'I' – centred will has gone. Speed destroys the human will. Moreover, a serious consequence of speed use is that, eventually, it causes psychopathological syndromes, specifically and so-called 'speed psychosis', and also paranoia. This occurs because of the forced entry into consciousness of the released etheric forces from the will sphere

## Cocaine

This is also the case with *cocaine*.

This poison, made synthetically from the leaves of the coca plant, releases etheric forces from the metabolic organs, and connects them with the limbs. Lungs and heart are over-stimulated as well, and this is why the Indians of the Andes have used these leaves for centuries to improve their stamina. An excessive dose, however, causes acute danger to life because of respiratory arrest and circulating failure. But more than anything else, the released etheric forces from the will sphere enormously intensify the thought activities. This is materialistic, purely intellectual thought, which is totally inaccessible to any spiritual content. The head feels like an overloaded telephone switchboard. Associations are made in a flash – it is fast, clean, and clear. This feels good. The addiction is in the head. Because of the surplus of forces of will the user feels sure of himself, has an inflated sense of self, is much bolder. Cocaine inflates the ego. One feels more powerful and confident – at parties, or during business meetings in situations of uncertainty. This semblance of a sense of self-assurance is a great temptation for anyone who wants to hide his own uncertainty or his feelings of inferiority. This is why cocaine is becoming more and more popular among teens and young adults.

What one loses, however, is real feelings, including the experience of one's own uncertainty, the tension, and the fear that the ego has to confront in order to grow. In their stead one has the hard, cold, steely and cynical feeling caused by cocaine. Compassionate and sensitive feeling is rendered impossible bcause the released etheric forces give such an overpowering experience of will power that the sensitive, spiritual, and truly emotional human element is overpowered. All that is nonsense! *No nonsense*; that is cocaine.

**Marijuana/hashish**

And *marijuana/hashish?*
This drug acts more subtly. Where does marijuana/hashish go in the human body?

By means of ECGs and radioactively labelled marijuana/hashish it has been discovered that the active components end up in: a) the brain, where they remain for some time; b) the rhythmic system, particularly the lungs and lymph system, which reduces immunity: c) the metabolism, including the sexual organs (4).

In all of these regions, and therefore in the total human being, toxic effects occur, which again result in the well known loosening of the ether body from the physical body. Accordingly, all of the partial death processes occurring with LSD arise with cannabis as well, although to a lesser extent. These include the release of emotions and memories, abnormally intense sense impressions, disorientation in space and time floating, going out. etc. And again, the unreliable conscious awareness of these experiences by way of the so-called distorting mirror are the result of the physical and etheric bodies no longer fitting together harmoniously (see the part on LSD). Marijuana/hashish has less of a 'kick', but works more subtly on the mutual relations of the human sheaths. That is why the term 'soft drugs' is used.

If we want more fully to understand the action of marijuana/hashish, we have to get a picture of the hemp plant, from which it is derived.

Hemp is an annual plant, which has an affinity particularly with the air and warmth elements. It is an airy plant of light. The wind looks after pollination. Its 'upper' part (with flowers and seed) dominates over the 'lower' part (leaves and roots): Light ether and warmth ether prevail over chemical and life ethers. Even in the leaves the activity of the light- and warmth ether is noticeable, with the stems radiating outwards, and the surface of the leaves tending to become slightly silicic (light ether). The leaves form a resin and fragrant oils (warmth ether).‡

This means there is a strong association with the astral sphere, which wafts around the plant. It is attracted to the cosmic-astral world. Thus it provides an ideal food for air animals: birds, which 'waft' around the earth, love hemp seed.

When the human being ingests marijuana/hashish, his or her consciousness (astral body) is invited, as it were, to get in touch with the cosmic – astral world. This is the same world in which our astral body dwells during sleep. The user, however, remains awake. He enters a kind of intermediate state between sleeping and waking – a sort of dream state. The marijuana/hashish user leaves his clearly awake consciousness behind and enters a kind of dreamy consciousness, which is experienced as pleasant and sweet due to the partial experience of the sleepy side of consciousness. With the use of opium this is even more the case.

Rudolf Steiner described this experience as follows:

> '. . . for he then occupies his body (with the use of opium) in such a way that he sleeps while being awake. This is why he can enjoy feelings of sweetness: this is very agreeable. It is as if the etheric body is permeated with sugar, a special kind of sugar, sweet through and through. At the same time the astral body is free from the material body, and allows him to observe everything, although – in an indistinct way.'

Marijuana/hashish, therefore, also draws forth the astral body from the etheric body. Beside the gap between the physical body and the etheric body, a second gap opens up.

The effects, with repeated use, are radical:

a) For the poisoned brain: thinking becomes confused, associative, dreamy, and aimless: loss of memory occurs, and concentration diminished: so-called 'hash thought'.
b) For the rhythmic system: this bodily foundation for the life of feeling becomes poisoned, with the result that in the aftermath of use extreme emotions arise. This is where marijuana has a very strong effect. It *gives* feelings, colours within the soul – in

contradistinction to cocaine. But the development of a real emotional life, created by the 'I' from joy and sorrow, is altogether out of the question. When the drug has lost its effect, the emotional life is dull and grey. 'All of my feelings are grey,' says an habitual hash user who has the courage to own up to his own condition in between trips. No longer is he capable of vivid, sensitive feelings. That is why again and again he seeks refuge with marijuana/hashish, just to feel something. 'At least then something is happening.'

c) For the metabolic organs, as the bodily foundation of the will, the picture is similar; the user no longer being 'present' in the organs, with the result that all will power vanishes. Says a regular hash user: 'I do everything half-way . . .'.

To summarize: with the use of marijuana/hashish, two gaps open up between the human sheaths – one between the physical body and the etheric body (the user dies partially), and another gap between the etheric body and the astral body (the user dreams away).

The user is torn apart with respect to his sheaths, excarnates, and moves away from the earth.

Because of this 'partial death,' the physical body mineralizes in a way that is typical for marijuana/hashish: it becomes 'woody' (marijuana/hashish users can always be recognized by their 'wooden' motions). Because of the dreaming away, a turbidity of consciousness and a drying up of the soul functions of thinking, feeling, and willing occur. The ego can no longer use its instruments, and consequently has no view any more of its own real future. A wooden, dried out, grey old tree in a foggy landscape – that is what the marijuana/hashish user turns himself into.

**Heroin**

*Heroin* goes a further step on the ladder of excarnation of the sheaths. It not only poisons the physical body, but also drives the 'I' out of the astral body.

This is why inner development becomes impossible. All development comes to a halt.

Heroin attacks the core of the soul – the 'I'. Moreover, it expels all individual feelings of fear, shame, sorrow, emptyness, etc., while only instrumental, intellectual thinking remain possible.

The addict becomes entirely head (compare with cocaine), with an empty soul.

What remains is an astral body with imitated, unoriginal thinking, and externally adapted behaviour, drives, desires, etc. These eventually turn

the addict into a beast of prey, hunting for gratification available through heroin. (About the nature of addiction, see the contribution by Marko van Gerven.)

The excarnating effect of heroin can be recognized in the 'gesture' of the plant from which heroin is derived: *papaver somniferum*. When we compare this with the common poppy (*papaver rhos*), we can observe how the common poppy suddenly shoots into flower, with a violent scarlet, and how it rapidly 'burns itself out'. The flowers wilt within a few days. *Somniferum*, whose leaves rise like flames licking upwards along the stem, concentrates this fiery burning force in its sap – the milk sap of its immature fruit (5). Heroin is made by chemical means from this sap. Its use gives a tremendous sense of fire, of warmth (the so-called 'honeymoon'), which persists for months, and sometimes longer.

But the ego – as that part of the human being most closely related to the element of fire – is expelled by heroin. This, too, the plant shows in its gesture. For when the milky sap, 'charged' with fire and warmth, is formed, then at that particular moment *somniferum* starts to withdraw from the earth. Its root formation diminishes, as can be seen in the accompanying series of photographs.

Or, as Jochen Bockemühl expresses it: 'The root activity ceases rapidly. This means that the plant withdraws from the salt process (earth) while pushing its forces upward in the sap.' (5)

At the moment the poppy seizes the ego with its fiery burning forces, at that moment it withdraws from the earth, excarnates. It takes the ego with it. With the use of heroin, the ego is forced out of the soul, leaving

53

behind a gaping hole between it and its instrument and carrier, the soul.
Heroin is an attack on the 'I'. Its victim is left with an empty soul.

## Alcohol

*Alcohol*, too, has an effect on the human ego. We know that this poison ends up especially in the rhythmic system (specifically in the blood circulation), but also in the liver and brain. (7)

The human ego, which has its bodily foundation in the blood, is also expelled in this case (alcohol dispels one's cares), with the result that the lower self gains the upper hand.

It is also typical of alcohol that the astral body becomes excessively bound to the bodily nature, with the result that the alcohol user materializes, hardens, becomes inaccessible for the spiritual element.

For children, the use of alcohol is especially damaging. According to Rudolf Steiner, 'because the grape vine already contains astrality, the child, when it drinks alcohol too early, acquires an astral body, which it should bring to full development only at age 14 or 15. It has no control over this premature astral body. The reason alcohol is so damaging for the child is that under the influence of alcohol it acquires an astral body of its own right away'.(2)

## Conclusion

The use of drugs almost always causes 'gaps' between the human sheaths. Between which sheaths the gap is forced, or which gap is emphasized, is different for each drug, as I have described as best I can. Via these gaps certain beings gain access to the human being. Lievegoed mentions ahrimanic beings in connection with LSD and other hallucinogens, and luciferic elemental beings for opium (6). Olav Koob mentions vampire beings in the case of heroin. (8) This is a serious problem, not only for the (ex-) user, but also for the helper. Here, too, much research is yet to be done.

In general, we can say that because of drug use the physical body mineralizes, and the etheric body becomes exhausted. The soul functions of thinking, feeling, and willing become paralyzed, and the ego loses its impulse for development and its sense of purpose because it is forced out. The human being dies in body and soul; spiritual development comes to a halt.

Is this excarnation, this death, this path away from the earth toward death compatible with incarnation, the development towards life, towards the earth, which the pupil experiences in school? Of course not!

*Regular drug use and individual development are, in my view, incompatible.*
Users who started at age fourteen and continue as users for twelve years (for instance on hashish), are at twenty six older than twenty six physically, yet psychologically they are still at fourteen. They still have to pass through virtually their entire puberty and adolescence. Little development has occurred in the astral body, soul, and ego.

A criterion for whether or not it is meaningful to keep a drug-using child in school lies in my view in the answer to the question of whether individual–personal development is still taking place.

† The reader may wish to refer to Appendix I, *The Elements of Human Life*, by Dr. Derek Blincow, for a full explanation of terms such as 'human sheaths', 'etheric body' and 'astral body'.

‡ When speaking of the etheric forces, these are again differentiated in themselves; into the warmth, light, chemical (on tone), and life ethers. See E.Lehrs, *Man or Matter*, Faber & Faber.

**References**

1. W. Bühler   *Bewusstseinserveiterung mit der Droge?* Studien und Versuche, 1972 Verlag Freies Geistesleben,Gmb H Stuttgart.

2. R. Steiner   *Nature en Mens*, geesteswetenschappelÿh beschouwd. 1978 Uitgeverij Vrij Grestesleven-Zeist.

3   Grohmann   *The Plant*, Lanthorn Press.

4.   Pelikan, *Heilpflanzenkunde*.

5.   Jochen Bockemühl   *Levensprocessen in de natuur*, Urtg. Vrij Grestesleven Zeist 1982.

6.   Bernard Lievegoed   *Man on The Threshold*, Hawthorn Press, Stroud 1983.

7.   J. H. van Epen   *De drugs van de wereld, de wereld van de drugs.* Staflen's wetenschappelÿhe uitgevers – maatschappÿ BV. Ulphen aan den Rÿn – Brussel 1981.

8.   Olaf Koob   *Droge und Suchtentstehung Soziale Hygiene.* Uitg. Verein für ein erweitertes Heilwesen e.v. 7263 Bad Liebenzell/Ul. 1981

9.   Rudolf Treichler   *Die Entwicklung der Seele im Lebenslauf*. Stuttgart: Verlag Freies Geistesleben 1981. To be published by Hawthorn Press in 1988–89.

# Appendix 1

# The Elements of Human Life

*Dr. Derek Blincow*

**1. The Four-fold Picture of the Human Being:**

Rudolf Steiner spoke of the human being developing in space and through time by way of the successive generation and elaboration of various 'sheaths'. Of these sheaths, he discriminated four members, each governed by a quite distinct set of laws.

He described a physical part, subject to physical laws, which we mould and fashion into our *physical body*. This we work on most dynamically during the earliest years of infancy and childhood, but this activity continues on into adulthood in an attenuated form. At death we discard our physical instrument, and it becomes subject totally to physical laws and thereby decomposes as the corpse. In life this body is directly influenced, sculpted, renewed, and held back from this decomposition process by what he described as 'formative forces'.

The 'etheric' or 'formative forces' are active throughout life but are perhaps most clearly seen in the young child when the physical body is being built up. As this process develops and reaches maturity some of these etheric forces gradually emancipate themselves from this primary task and become available as cognitive capacities. The human being organizes these disparate groups of forces into a coherent and individualized entity at about the time of the second dentition when we can speak of the birth of the *etheric body*.†

The physical and etheric bodies work closely together but have quite different affinities. While the physical shares the characteristics of the mineral realm and has its point of contact via the gravity-bound material world, the etheric altogether flaunts such constraints. It works in the streaming fluids of the body, works to renew and restore the disintegrating physical, lives according to levity. The plant realm, with its striving away from the earth, is a picture of the activity of the etheric in the natural world. In the human being we see the purest collaboration of physical and etheric in the sleeping state. When we awake another and quite different principle appears.

Working around and into this physical and etheric constitution are forces which have their point of contact in the medium of air. These 'astral' forces are active indirectly via the maternal organism in the embryonic life, enter more directly at birth as true respiration commences, and are step by step drawn deeper into the organism between the second dentition and puberty. The *astral body* is born at puberty bringing with it sexual maturity and quite new faculties of human feeling. Sexuality and a psychological richness and complexity may at first be bewildering and reveal themselves in new extremes of emotional states. A certain maturity has been achieved but it is still searching for a core identity.

However that identity – the individuality which hovers over this early development, does not work fully from within until the years of late adolescence. From then on the process intensifies as the will takes a more directed role in psychological development, focussing capacities and preparing future possibilities of soul and spiritual development (see section 3 below). This human individualizing function belongs to the ego, whose thrust comes directly through human warmth, that is, warmth interpreted in a not too physical way. To summarize:

        Physical . . . . . . . . . . . . . . . . . . . . . . . . . Earth (gravity)
        Etheric . . . . . . . . . . . . . . . . . . . . . . . . . . Water (levity)
        Astral . . . . . . . . . . . . . . . . . . . . . . . . . . . . . . . . . Air
        Ego . . . . . . . . . . . . . . . . . . . . . . . . . . . . . . . . . Warmth

If we go further to characterise the astral realm as shared alike by the animal kingdom, whereas we are truly and fully human only in our ego development, we have the schema:

        Physical . . . . . . . . . . . . . . . . . . . . . . . . . . . . . Mineral
        Physical. Etheric . . . . . . . . . . . . . . . . . . . . . . . . . Plant
        Physical. Etheric. Astral . . . . . . . . . . . . . . . . . . . Animal
        Physical. Etheric. Astral. Ego . . . . . . . . . . . . . . . Human

We have in effect a four-fold picture of the human being related on the one hand to the elements and also on the other to the various realms of nature.

## 2. Three-fold Man

It was a main contribution of Rudolf Steiner to follow the interweaving of these four principles (we could also say 'humours', or 'temperaments' to reflect the ancestry of these qualities) into the phenomenology of the human being as a whole. This whole he saw as the joint effect of three distinct systems each with its own and characteristic admixture of elementary principles.

Concentrated predominantly in the region of the head there is the upper or *nerve-sense pole*, and from there extending over the whole organism, particularly over its surfaces, skin, and appendages. This has primarily to do with stable form, the sensory activity based on this, and capacities for thinking and a clear consciousness. Here processes have come to rest, achieved a certain hardness and mineralisation, are more or less passive reflectors of both internal and external events. Steiner characterised this pole as tending inherently to '*sclerosis*' and left to its own devices it would convey this influence to the rest of the organism, resulting in the variety of sclerotic illnesses.

Diametrically opposite in effect is the activity of the *metabolic-limb* system. Found mainly in the abdominal cavity and in the work of the limbs it functions to transform both the inner and outer world. While the nerve sense pole presents a crystalline fixity, the metabolic limb man is constantly in process, dissolving and reforming structures, disintegrating matter and building up dynamically moulded substance. The nerve-sense pole thinks, the metabolic-limb system wills, and wills in and through the production of those same forces seen at work in '*inflammation*'. Were the metabolism to overflow its bounds, fever, its natural tendency, would ensue.

Fever versus sclerosis, each pole representing potential illness, each also reflecting the different poles of human life. For the common illnesses of childhood are predominantly the feverish, metabolic type (e.g. measles etc.), of adulthood, certainly in the modern industrialized societies such as ours, sclerosing (e.g. arteriosclerosis)

We can now see how the four members already referred to (see section 1 above) work differently in the two systems. The warmth relationships for example are quite distinct, and insofar as the tendency towards fever manifests through an overabundance of metabolism, just so far has the ego become the more intensively engaged in that region. Likewise, but in a contrary manner, to the extent to which we can bring another kind of warmth into our thinking, to that extent precisely is our ego engaged in the head. The fluid organisation presents a vivid picture of this dichotomy; the etheric forces can engage in a mobile and active way in the surging fluid life of the lower region, while it is to a certain degree released and disengaged from the tranquil and relative stillness of the cerebrospinal fluid. Here and thus does thinking become possible; calm, clear, and ordered. All four principles work into the three-fold human being to give a picture of surprising complexity and discrimination.

Yet, were we to be merely split between these poles we should be constantly ill and incapable of concerted action. To become a 'thinking doer'‡ there arises from early on in our embryonic life a middle system whose activity is carried out in rhythms. This rhythmic system extends throughout the organism but has its organic realisation in the region of the chest, manifested in the inherent rhythmicity of the heart and lung. It is above all a mediator, turning at the one instant to the upper pole, and in the next to the lower. The movement of the heart demonstrates in itself this rhythmic oscillation between engorgement with blood (inflamed) in diastole, and the contracted form (sclerosed) of systole. This semi-conscious equilibration, as it proceeds, becomes the basis for our life of feeling.

If nerve-sense and metabolic-limb lead over into differing forms of pathology, the rhythmic system could be seen to be a dynamic healing agent for the human condition:

Nerve-sense . . . . . Upper Pole . . . . Thinking . . . . . Sclerosis
Rhythmic . . . . . . . Middle . . . . . . Feeling . . . . . . Healing
Metabolic-limb . . . Lower Pole . . . . Willing . . . . . . Inflammation

## 3. Soul and Spiritual Development

Human maturation is for Steiner a long and life-long question. For as the bodily organization reaches a certain fulfillment, forces become available and undergo their own development in the psychological and spiritual domains.

Building upon the already mentioned births of physical, etheric, astral bodies and the advent of the ego working from within, Steiner drew attention to the continued working of the ego, the individuality, within the established soul functions. And he went further to place individual development within the wider context of the evolution of humanity as a whole.

In individual terms, during the years approx. 21–28, we develop the 'sentient soul', from age 28–35 the 'intellectual soul', and after the age of 35 the 'consciousness soul'.

In our time and dating from the Renaissance in Europe, humanity has been unfolding the new possibilities of the consciousness soul. With the gradual dying away of the inherited values of the medieval world, man faces a manifestly objective reality, but one in which meaning is no longer certain. Science arises upon the basis of a radical doubt, a perspective from which to observe, survey, reflect upon a material world whose laws we can discern and manipulate. This is a rigorous scepticism that estranges man from a universe he once felt as home. It is a time of crisis where the intellect rules but can not provide.

A new and consciously spiritual principle has then to be grasped, and grasped by the free individual will. For in order to fully comprehend our situation as human beings we have to go beyond the objective appearance and apprehend a world of non-material forces, processes, and ultimately beings of a decidedly spiritual nature. As such the challenge is to carry over an objective methodology into the perception and investigation of this spiritual world – a 'spiritual science'.

Steiner inaugurated 'anthroposophy', literally anthropos = man, sophia = wisdom, as the vehicle for this work, for he contended that by the end of the present century many would begin to have direct experience of a spiritual nature for which they would neither have the concepts nor adequate preparation.* He called such experiences 'crossing the threshold', previously guarded and secure to all but select groups, and now opening to mankind as a whole. The potential for a leap in human development confronts us in the same measure as the alarming possibility that we should fail to use, or misuse, such capacities. Then would arise a total materialism, whose appeal has become so entrancing in our time.

## POSTSCRIPT

I hope that the foregoing account will provide some background to this book. It is of necessity brief, and partial, and those more acquainted with Steiner and an anthroposophical approach must be painfully aware of its shortcomings. There may also appear in the text terms which I will not have covered, and I have attempted to provide some explanatory background by way of footnotes. A bibliography of relevant works by Steiner follows at the end of the book.

Nevertheless, if I have stressed too much the deficiencies, I also hope that readers, both stimulated or horrified, will be inspired to take up the challenge of the original. I am pleased to introduce to you work that has done just that, and forged a workable and illuminating path through this dark and desperate chapter of our modern life.

Dr. Derek Blincow
London 1986.

† Also called the 'life body' or 'body of formative forces' amongst other terms, '*Theosophy*' by R. Steiner for a more detailed introduction to these members.

‡ A concept Steiner employs to characterise the object of his '*Philosophy of Freedom*'.

\* For the outline of a preparatory method Steiner offered, see '*Knowledge of the Higher Worlds and its Attainment*'.

# Appendix II
# Contacts

The local drugline, drug advice centre, citizens advice bureau will assist you in finding useful sources of help – in the form of information, counselling, educational talks, etc.

*ARTA* itself can be contacted at Krakelingweg 25, 3703 HP Zeist, Netherlands (05220-55759).

There is an initiative to plan a similar venture in the U.K. known as the St Brendan Group

# Books from Hawthorn Press

## Social Ecology Series

### ARIADNE'S AWAKENING
### Taking up the threads of consciousness.
Margli Matthews, Signe Schaefer and Betty Staley.

Much has been written about women and men in terms of role, gender and social forms through the ages. The past two decades have witnessed widespread change in 'rights' and 'equality' on external levels, but this has not always made for more human fulfilment. The authors acknowledge the context of feminism, but broaden its picture enormously. They view 'masculine' and 'feminine' not just as bodily forms, but as principles of meaning: principles at work within each of us, in society and indeed in the entire span of Earth Evolution.

*Ariadne's Awakening* traces through myth and history the journey humankind has made up to the present; it considers phases of life, relationships for men and women, and confronts such issues as the scientific management of conception and death, the rape of Earth's natural resources and the need for a New Feminine to influence values and decisions for the future.

*Ariadne's Awakening* is a book about understanding ourselves, and a search for a creative balance.

Signe Schaefer teaches at the Waldorf Institute, Spring Valley, New York. Margli Matthews teaches at Emerson College, Sussex and Betty Staley teaches in California. Signe and Margli were founder members of the Ariadne Women's Group, and wrote articles for *Lifeways*.

210 × 135mm; sewn limp bound; 224pp; ISBN I 869 890 01 9.
To be published in German and Dutch.

### VISION IN ACTION
### The art of taking and shaping initiatives.
Christopher Schaefer and Tijno Voors.

*Vision* is a working book for those involved in taking and shaping initiatives.
The authors ask:
How can individuals ang groups take initiatives successfully? Once started, how can projects be shaped and developed effectively?

Building on their practical experience of fostering and taking initiatives, the authors offer useful road maps to those developing ventures. Examples are given of community projects, schools, exployment initiatives, small business, farms, cultural and therapeutic centres.

The road maps include: the process of starting and nurturing initiatives; ways of working together, financing initiatives; the development phases of initiatives; initiatives and individual development.

There are exercises, case studies and questionnaires which can be used by people preparing and reviewing initiatives, or considering their next step.

Christopher Schaefer PhD works in social and community development in the USA. Tijno Voors works at the centre for Social Development at Emerson College, Sussex.

210 × 135mm; sewn limp bound; 224pp; 3 illustrations; Publication date 1st September 1986; ISBN 0 950 706 29 9. Not for sale in the U.S.A.

# RECOGNITION OF REALITY
## Reflections and prose poems.
## Adam Curle.

Those of us living in the modern Western world (or 'North') have daily access to visual and factual images which travel with unprecedented rapidity from their place of origin to our newspaper page or television screen. Seemingly, these aim to 'inform' us about contemporary war, famine, poverty, summit meetings, human suffering, or other newsworthy events. How much of this we actually digest or comprehend is another matter. For many it is often enough to grapple with understanding our individual positions here and now, at this time, during this event or in this moment. And yet we are part of a wider world.

Adam Curle's mediation work over the past twenty-two years has taken him to international and personal situations of great tension, despair, hope, pain and change. Previous to and during this period he has been involved in problems of Third World Development and has held professorships in psychology, education, development and peace studies at Exeter, Ghana, Harvard and Bradford Universities.

But in *Recognition of Reality* he chooses not to lecture. This is a book of reflections; glimpses of inner and outer worlds caught in poetic form and always based on true experience. At times gentle, at times painful, these pieces combine to offer our Age a compassionate interpretation of reality, and vision for the future. *Recognition of Reality* seeks to convey the essential truth and spiritual essence so often distorted or unseen amid human suffering and despair. Only by coming to terms with our fundamental being will we succeed in transforming and renewing this earth.

210 × 135mm; paperback; 100pp approx; 67 poems; Publication in late Autumn 1987.

# DYING FORESTS
## A crisis in consciousness.
## Transforming our way of life.
## 46 colour pictures and text by Jochen Bockemühl.
## Introduction by Professor Brian Goodwin. Translated by John Meeks.

Forests are dying in central Europe – many trees are dying in the Swiss mountains, threatening erosion problems. Many lakes in Scandinavia, Scotland and North Wales now have no fish. Sulphur dioxide, ozone, nitric oxides from industry, traffic and power stations are some causes. But what part do people play in causing forest die-back?

*Dying Forests* offers the insights of Jochen Bockemühl – both scientist and artist – into the underlying causes of forest die–back.

The author, by means of his water colour sketches and commentary, describes how, through the development of a sensitive observation of landscape ecology, a more conscious encounter with nature can take place. Through the exercises described in *Dying Forests*, the strength to change one's habits and our destructive technology may emerge. *Dying Forests* is a striking example of the use of Geothe's scientific method which aims to understand the living whole, rather than the dead parts.

Jochen Bockemühl is a scientist working at Goetheanum Research Laboratory in Dornack, Switzerland. He has lectured and conducted many 'observation workshops' in the English speaking world. His work on plant metamorphosis is included in Open University biology course texts.

Full colour cover; 210 × 210mm; sewn limp bound; 96pp; 46 water colour illustrations in full colour, plus drawings; ISBN 1 869 890 02 7.

## RUDOLF STEINER
Life, work, inner path and social initiatives.
Rudi Lissau.

This book gives a vivid picture of Rudolf Steiner's life and work. It aims to point out the relevance of Steiner's activities to contemporary social and human concerns. There are chapters on Steiner's philosophy; his view of the universe, earth and the human being; Christ and human destiny; the meditative path; education and social development; approaches to Rudolf Steiner's work and obstacles.

Rudi Lissau has taught adolescents at Wynstones School for over forty years. He has written and lectured widely in North America, the UK, Scandinavia and Central Europe.

*A very lucid, warm hearted and judicious account of anthrosophy which I read with pleasure and gratitude.*
                                                                Saul Bellow.

210 × 135mm; 192pp approx; sewn limp bound; Publication date 1st September 1987; ISBN 1 869 890 06 X.

### Plus

**Man on the Threshold,** B C J Lievegoed, *pb*

**Social Ecology,** M Large, *pb*

**If you have difficulties ordering from a bookshop you can order direct from Hawthorn Press, Bankfield House, 13 Wallbridge, Stroud, Glos. GL5 3JA (04536) 77040.**